The Legal Writing Handbook

Practice Book
Sixth Edition

Aspen Coursebook Series

The Legal Writing Handbook

Practice Book
Sixth Edition

Laurel Currie Oates
Anne Enquist

Wolters Kluwer
Law & Business

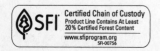

About Wolters Kluwer Law & Business

Wolters Kluwer Law & Business is a leading global provider of intelligent information and digital solutions for legal and business professionals in key specialty areas, and respected educational resources for professors and law students. Wolters Kluwer Law & Business connects legal and business professionals as well as those in the education market with timely, specialized authoritative content and information-enabled solutions to support success through productivity, accuracy and mobility.

Serving customers worldwide, Wolters Kluwer Law & Business products include those under the Aspen Publishers, CCH, Kluwer Law International, Loislaw, ftwilliam.com and MediRegs family of products.

CCH products have been a trusted resource since 1913, and are highly regarded resources for legal, securities, antitrust and trade regulation, government contracting, banking, pension, payroll, employment and labor, and healthcare reimbursement and compliance professionals.

Aspen Publishers products provide essential information to attorneys, business professionals and law students. Written by preeminent authorities, the product line offers analytical and practical information in a range of specialty practice areas from securities law and intellectual property to mergers and acquisitions and pension/benefits. Aspen's trusted legal education resources provide professors and students with high-quality, up-to-date and effective resources for successful instruction and study in all areas of the law.

Kluwer Law International products provide the global business community with reliable international legal information in English. Legal practitioners, corporate counsel and business executives around the world rely on Kluwer Law journals, looseleafs, books, and electronic products for comprehensive information in many areas of international legal practice.

Loislaw is a comprehensive online legal research product providing legal content to law firm practitioners of various specializations. Loislaw provides attorneys with the ability to quickly and efficiently find the necessary legal information they need, when and where they need it, by facilitating access to primary law as well as state-specific law, records, forms and treatises.

ftwilliam.com offers employee benefits professionals the highest quality plan documents (retirement, welfare and non-qualified) and government forms (5500/PBGC, 1099 and IRS) software at highly competitive prices.

MediRegs products provide integrated health care compliance content and software solutions for professionals in healthcare, higher education and life sciences, including professionals in accounting, law and consulting.

Wolters Kluwer Law & Business, a division of Wolters Kluwer, is headquartered in New York. Wolters Kluwer is a market-leading global information services company focused on professionals.

Table of Contents

Preface

Practice makes perfect, or so they say. For some learners, reinforcement of a concept by using it in new contexts is exactly what they need to master the concept. For this reason, we have written *The Legal Writing Handbook, The Practice Book, Sixth Edition.*

From its title, it should be obvious that this Practice Book was designed to accompany and supplement *The Legal Writing Handbook, Sixth Edition.* The exercise numbers match the chapter numbers in *The Legal Writing Handbook, Sixth Edition.* Users of *Just Writing, Fourth Edition* will also find that the Practice Book is a supplement to that text. Although the exercise numbers do not match the chapter numbers in *Just Writing, Fourth Edition,* users should be able to match the exercises to the appropriate chapters by the wording in the chapter and exercise titles.

The Writing Exercises have an accompanying set of Answers at the back of the book. The Answers to each exercise are in the second column in the table of contents. Many of the Answers are annotated so that readers can better understand why a given answer is correct. Our hope is that by providing the Answers, this portion of the book becomes self-teaching.

The Writing Exercises have been used with hundreds of our own students over the years. We have appreciated their feedback on the exercises and have modified many based on their comments. In addition, many of the sample sentences were taken directly from our own students' writing. For their willingness to allow us to use their sample writing in this book, we especially want to thank these students.

The Authors

Note: there are no exercises for Chapters 1-21. Exercises previously in the Practice Book have been incorporated into the sixth edition of the Legal Writing Handbook.

Chapter 22
Effective Paragraphs

This exercise should be done after reading Section 22.4 in the *Handbook.*

Read the following paragraph from an appellate brief and decide if it should be broken up into shorter paragraphs and, if so, where.

There are some limited exceptions to the prohibitive rule stated in the above cases; however, the facts of the present case do not fall into those exceptions. The first exception allows the questioning of a witness about religious beliefs when those beliefs are relevant to some issue other than the credibility of the witness. *State v. Stone*, 728 P.2d 674 (Ariz. Ct. App. 1986). In the present case, Ms. Patten's religious activities and beliefs were not at issue and the only conceivable purpose that the prosecution could have had for questioning her about them was to bolster her credibility by impressing the jury with her religiousness. The second exception applies when reference to the religious beliefs of a witness is isolated and not significant to the trial proceedings in their entirety. *Id.* at 871, 728 P.2d at 678. In the present case, the prosecution's questions--over repeated objections--about Ms. Patten's religious beliefs, as well as the closing argument comments about those beliefs, cannot be deemed isolated and inadvertent. (RP 151-52, 186). Under the third exception, inquiry about the religious beliefs of a witness will not give rise to constitutional error if the assigning party invites the error. *People v. Baseer*, 90 Ill. App. 3d 866, 414 N.E.2d 5 (1980). Hence, when a defendant testifies as to his own religious beliefs in an attempt to bolster his credibility, he will not be heard to complain when the prosecution cross-examines him about his beliefs. *Id.* at 871, 414 N.E.2d at 10. In the present case, Mr. Davidson's counsel never attempted to question Ms. Patten about her religious beliefs so as to affect her credibility, so it cannot be said that the defense "opened the door" to the prosecution's questioning of Ms. Patten about her religious beliefs. *Id.* In short, none of the exceptions apply. Therefore, the trial court's allowance of the prosecution's questioning was an error of constitutional magnitude.

EXERCISE 22B: PARAGRAPH LENGTH

This exercise should be done after reading Section 22.4 in the *Handbook.*

Read the following statement of facts and decide if the paragraphs are the appropriate length. Rewrite and re-paragraph as needed.

Statement of Facts

Four neighbors--Mr. and Mrs. Archer, Mr. Baker, Mr. and Ms. Carlisle, and Ms. DeLeon--live adjacent to the Urban High School athletic field. They have asked us to represent them in a lawsuit against the Seattle School Board.

You have asked me to research their claim and determine whether they have a cause of action in nuisance and trespass.

Despite several neighbors' complaints, the Metropolitan School Board has allowed Say No to Drugs (SND) baseball games to be played at Urban High on Tuesday and Thursday from 8 p.m. to midnight. The SND program, aimed at local drug users, has been very successful and has attracted nationwide attention. Four neighbors living adjacent to the Urban High athletic field--Mr. and Mrs. Archer, Mr. Baker, Mr. and Mrs. Carlisle, and Mrs. DeLeon--have filed suit against the school district in Washington State Superior Court, Puget Sound County. These neighbors seek to enjoin baseball at Urban High between the hours of 9:30 p.m. and midnight. They also seek monetary compensation for damages resulting from nuisance and trespass.

Mr. and Mrs. Archer, an elderly couple, compete in growing roses. Before September 1987, the Archers had approximately 20 rosebushes, most of which were budding. Since September, four of their bushes have been destroyed. In

22-4

addition, so many buds have been damaged that the Archers will be unable to enter any rose competitions this season. The Archers allege that baseball players trespassing across their property have caused the damage.

Mr. Baker, a night court judge who works from 5 p.m. to 1 a.m., has had two picture windows and a valuable vase broken by baseballs.

The Carlisles are a young couple with an 18-month-old daughter. The lights and noise from the night baseball prevent their daughter from sleeping until 12:30 a.m. Although these disturbances to her sleep occur only twice a week, the Carlisles claim that the loss of sleep interrupts the baby's entire weekly schedule.

Mrs. DeLeon, a stockbroker, wakes at 5 a.m. to be at work by 7 a.m. Lately, she has been irritable at work. Her job performance has suffered, and tranquilizers have not helped. Mrs. DeLeon alleges her problem is her inability to sleep because of the lights and noise from the night baseball. She claims that if the night baseball continues, she will have to sell her home at a loss.

No baseballs or baseball players have entered the Carlisles' or Mrs. DeLeon's property. Both the Carlisles' and Mrs. DeLeon's property are protected by a high fence, but the school property itself is not fenced between the plaintiffs' property and the field.

Urban High's field is the only lighted baseball field within a ten-mile radius of Urban High.

EXERCISE 22C: TOPIC SENTENCES

This exercise should be done after reading Section 22.5.1 in the *Handbook*.

Read the following paragraphs and revise the topic sentences so that they 1) transition from the preceding paragraph, 2) introduce the new topic, and 3) assert something about the new topic.

1.　Even though the more current cases adopt a liberal reading, there are cases that support a motion to quash service. These cases limit *Rovinski* by recognizing that "it is not enough to have actual notice. In *Frasca*, for example, service of process was left with defendant's daughter-in-law in Pennsylvania. The defendant, who did receive actual notice, had lived in Massachusetts for fifty years and had visited his son in Pennsylvania only twice during that time. *Id.* at 269.

2. In order to use *Frasca* to support our client, we must characterize Ms. Clay-Poole's trips to California as visits. She stayed only three or four days at a time. The possessions she kept in California were not enough for even a three or four day visit, so she had to carry additional belongings with her. By demonstrating that her contacts with the California residence were minimal, we can show that her husband's home was not her "dwelling house or usual place of abode."

3. The plaintiff will point out the factual differences between our case and *Frasca*. Frasca was clearly a visitor in Pennsylvania. He apparently did not travel there with any regularity. He had only been at the house two times in the past fifty years. Our client travels to California regularly, keeps clothing at the house, and receives mail addressed to her and her husband there. Her contacts are more extensive.

4. Concerning element number one, was Smith a member of the ADEA protected class at the time of his discharge? At the time of Smith's discharge, ADEA applied only to individuals who were at least forty years old but less than seventy years old. 29 U.S.C. § 631(a) (1982). Because Smith was forty-nine years old when he was discharged, he was within the ADEA protected class. Therefore, element number one is satisfied.

This exercise should be done after reading Section 22.5.3 in the *Handbook*.

Find the topic sentence and concluding sentence in the following paragraph. Discuss whether the topic sentence signals to the reader the key point that the paragraph will make and whether the concluding sentence is helpful to the reader.

A good illustration of the court awarding damages for inconvenience and annoyance is *Riblet v. Spokane-Portland Cement Co.*, 45 Wash. 2d 346, 274 P.2d 574 (1954). In *Riblet*, the plaintiffs were able to recover for the annoyance and inconvenience caused by cement dust. Although the dust itself was imperceptible "as is usually the case when nuisance involves dust, gas, smoke, noise, etc.," the dust's effects disrupted the ordinary activities of family life. Consequently, the annoyance was compensable. *Id.*

EXERCISE 22E: PARAGRAPH BLOCKS

This exercise should be done after reading Section 22.6 in the *Handbook*.

Read the following discussion section of a memo. Although the law has changed since this memo was written, the memo demonstrates how topic paragraphs and paragraph blocks fit together. Mark the topic paragraphs for paragraph blocks and the topic sentences for individual paragraphs.

Discussion

"Actual physical control" is governed by a statute that states in part: "It is unlawful . . . for any person who is under the influence of alcohol to . . . be in actual physical control of a motor vehicle upon the ways of this state open to the public." Mont. Code Ann. § 61.8.4011)(a) (1983). Generally, three elements of the statute bear examination: 1) the person must be under the influence of alcohol; 2) the person must be in actual physical control of a motor vehicle; and 3) the motor vehicle must be on the ways of Montana that are open to the public.

Under the Influence

Considering the fact pattern of the Renko case, the court will probably find that the question of whether Mr. Renko was under the influence of alcohol is not worthy of in-depth discussion. The results of the breathalyzer test, the vomit, and the testimony of the arresting officer establish that our client was legally intoxicated at the time of arrest, so the first element of the offense is not at issue.

Ways of the State

Although the primary issue of the case focuses upon resolving questions pertaining to actual physical control, the issue of whether Mr. Renko's truck was on the ways of the state open to the public deserves brief analysis. The traffic code states that "'ways of the state open to the public' means any highway, road, alley lane, parking area, or other public or private place adapted and fitted for public travel that is in common use by the public." Mont. Code Ann. § 61.8.101(1)(1983). The language specifically states "adapted and fitted for public travel." Since Mr. Renko's truck was found on the shoulder, the court would have to determine whether the shoulder of a highway is adapted and fitted for public travel. In defining other statutory language, the Montana Supreme Court resorted to dictionary definitions. Webster defines shoulder as "either edge of a roadway; specifically: the part of the roadway *outside the traveled way*" (emphasis added). It is possible, then, that the court could interpret the statutory language narrowly and conclude that the term "ways" does not encompass shoulders.

However, a narrow construction of the term "ways" is unlikely. In fact, there are two strong indications that Montana will favor a broad construction: 1) an extension stated in the statutory definition of "highway"; and 2) an interpretation of "ways" given in a Montana Supreme Court decision. By statutory definition, "[h]ighway means the entire width between the boundary lines of every publicly maintained way when any part thereof is open to the use of the public for purposes of vehicular travel, *except that for the purpose of chapter 8 the term also includes ways which have been or shall be dedicated to public use.*" (emphasis added) Mont. Code Ann. § 61.1.201 (1983). Chapter 8 includes offenses committed while under the influence of alcohol. Since the legislature expanded the statutory definition for alcohol-related offenses, it follows that the legislature intended to broaden, not narrow, the term. Following the legislature's lead, the Montana Supreme Court stipulated that "ways" encompasses state and county right-of-ways, including borrow pits, which road maintenance crews use as sources of dirt and gravel. *State v. Taylor,* 242 Mont. 43, 44, 661 P.2d 33, 34 (1983). It is highly unlikely that the court would include borrow pits but exempt shoulders from the term "ways." The court will probably conclude that Mr. Renko's truck was on the ways of the state open to the public.

Actual Physical Control

Although it is relatively easy to determine that the facts in this case satisfy the elements of "under the influence" and "on the ways," it is more difficult to decide whether they constitute "actual physical control" of a motor vehicle. The statute does not further explain "actual physical control," but the Montana Supreme Court supplied the following dictionary definition: "[I]t means existing or present bodily restraint, directing influence, domination or regulation of an automobile." *State v. Ruona*, 133 Mont. 243, 246, 321 P.2d 615, 618 (1958).

The elements of the definition have not been completely defined; however, the court has given some clarification. In *Ruona*, the court stated that "restraint" includes preventing a car from moving; movement of a vehicle is not necessary for actual physical control. 133 Mont. at 246, 321 P.2d at 618. The court further clarified the term "regulation" by asserting that a sleeping driver who remains behind the steering wheel of a vehicle "remains in a position to regulate" the vehicle and "has not relinquished control" of the vehicle. *Taylor*, 242 Mont. at 44, 661 P.2d 34. Regulation or control is not diminished by the fact that a vehicle is incapable of moving because, as previously noted, movement is not required. *Taylor*, 242 Mont. at 44, 661 P.2d at 34 (citing *Ruona*, 133 Mont. at 247, 321 P.2d at 619).

The Montana court has applied these definitions to cases with the following fact patterns: 1) the driver was asleep and intoxicated; 2) the driver was positioned behind the steering wheel of the motor vehicle; 3) the vehicle's motor was running; 4) the vehicle was parked; and 5) the vehicle was at least partially on the pavement of a roadway. In both of the leading Montana cases, the court held that the driver was in actual physical control of his vehicle. *Ruona*, 133 Mont. 243, 321 P.2d 615; *Taylor*, 242 Mont. 43, 661 P.2d 33. However, the court has not addressed the exact fact pattern presented by the Renko case.

The Renko fact pattern differs in the following respects: 1) the driver was not seated behind the steering wheel; 2) the engine of the vehicle was not running; and 3) the vehicle was not even partially on the traveled portion of the roadway. Although the "driver's position" may be considered separately, "engine not running" and "vehicle not on roadway" are closely related in terms of legal significance and should be analyzed together. In fact, the interrelationship of all three factors should be considered for two reasons. First, although a single factor may not affect the outcome of a case, the combination of that factor with others may be legally significant. Second, the combination of the aforementioned factors may be important in showing the defendant's intent.

Positioning in the driver's seat is a common element in all the national cases that have found actual physical control of a motionless vehicle, *State v. Smelter*, 36 Wash. App. 439, 441, 674 P.2d 690, 692 (1984), except for one Oklahoma case, *Hughes v. State*, 509 Okla., 157, 535 P.2d 1023 (1975) (Defendant was lying across the front seat but was awake and the vehicle was not only on the roadway but also at a 90 degree angle to the flow of traffic.) The theory behind the decisions is that an intoxicated person who is seated behind the steering wheel is still in a position to control the vehicle and could be considered a potential threat to the public. *Ruona*, 133 Mont. at 243, 321 P.2d at 619 (quoting *State v. Webb*, 78 Ariz. 8, 274 P.2d 338, (1954)).

The Montana court could view the positioning question in two ways: 1) it could hold that positioning behind the steering wheel is essential to manifest control of the vehicle, *Cincinnati v. Kelley*, 47 Ohio St. 2d 94, 351 N.E.2d 85 (1976); or 2) it could find that positioning is relatively unimportant because once awakened, a driver could quickly move behind the wheel and would pose as great a threat to society as the driver who remained behind the wheel while he slept. *State v. Bugger*, 25 Utah 2d 404, 483 P.2d 442, (1971) (Ellett, J., dissenting). Considering that the Montana court has focused on the idea that the purpose of the statute is to protect the public and has found that a sleeping, intoxicated driver is still a threat to the public, *Ruona*, 133 Mont. at 243, 321 P.2d at 619, the court would probably find that a sleeping, intoxicated driver who is lying on the front seat poses a potential threat to the public.

Because only a few cases have addressed the issues of whether actual physical control of a vehicle can be established when the engine is not running or when the vehicle is entirely off the traveled portion of the roadway, it is difficult to isolate these factors in terms of legal significance. Actual physical control has been found when the vehicle was legally parked and the engine was not running but when the driver was awake and in the driver's seat. *Kelley*, 47 Ohio St. 2d 94, 351 N.E.2d 85. In *Kelley*, the court noted that the defendant was behind the wheel, had possession of the key, and was in such a condition that he could have started the vehicle. 47 Ohio St. 2d 94, 351 N.E.2d 85.

In contrast, courts have been reluctant to find actual physical control when the driver has been found asleep in a vehicle that was legally parked on the shoulder of the roadway with the engine turned off. For example, in *State v. Bugger*, the Utah Supreme Court held that a defendant was not in actual physical control because he was not controlling the vehicle or exercising any dominion over it. *State v. Bugger*, 25 Utah 2d 404, 483 P.2d 442. In *State v. Zavala*, the Arizona Supreme Court held that a defendant had voluntarily relinquished control of the vehicle. *State v. Zavala*, 136 Ariz. 356, 666 P.2d 456 (1983). The Arizona court considered the voluntary action or intent of the driver important and wished to foster the policy of encouraging drunk drivers to pull out of traffic, to turn off the engine, and to go to sleep. *Zavala*, 136 Ariz. 356, 666 P.2d 456 (1983).

In short, before the Montana court can determine whether Mr. Renko was in actual physical control of the vehicle, the court must determine the following issues: 1) whether Mr. Renko had relinquished control of the vehicle; and 2) whether the Montana legislature intended to foster a policy of encouraging intoxicated drivers to pull off the road to sleep.

With regard to the first issue, other jurisdictions have partially defined "control" and "operate" in terms of the defendant's manipulation of mechanical or electrical apparatus. Cases that relate to such a definition have dealt with defendants who were awake and were attempting either to brake or to steer inoperable vehicles. *State v. Swift*, 125 Conn. 399, 6 A.2d 359 (1939); *State v. Storrs*, 105 Vt. 180, 163 A. 56 (1933). However, it is conceivable that a court, particularly one that is inclined to broadly construe traffic regulations concerning intoxicated drivers, could apply the "manipulation of mechanical and electrical apparatus" definition in the Renko case. The court could conclude that Mr. Renko's left foot was manipulating the brake pedal and illuminating the brake lights; therefore, he had not relinquished control of the vehicle. The court could reach the same conclusion by finding that Mr. Renko was using "present bodily restraint" to prevent the car from moving.

As a subissue in determining control, the court would have to address the question of whether operability is required. If it is not required, then no further discussion of this issue would be necessary; and in light of the Montana court's holding in *Taylor*, operability probably would not be required because movement is not required and the driver was still considered to be in actual physical control of a vehicle that he could not move. 242 Mont. at 43, 661 P.2d at 34.

If some form of operability is required, then the court must decide whether to focus on the defendant's ability to operate the vehicle or on the vehicle's condition. *State v. Smelter*, 36 Wash. App. 439, 444, 674 P.2d 690, 693 (1984). In focusing on the defendant's condition, the court could find that since the defendant had the key and was in the cab of the truck, he would have been able to operate the vehicle had he been awakened. Not only is it possible that he could have operated the truck, it is evident that he did drive the truck from the tavern to the freeway before parking it on the shoulder. In focusing on the vehicle's condition, the Washington court used the trial court's "reasonably operable" standard and defined that term as any malfunction short of a cracked block or a similar problem that would render the vehicle totally inoperable. *Smelter*, 36 Wash. App. at 444, 674 P.2d at 693. By that definition, Mr. Renko's truck was reasonably operable regardless of whether it would start. Therefore, if the Montana court considers operability an issue, it would probably find that Mr. Renko was capable of operating the vehicle and that the vehicle was in reasonably operable condition.

The second question, whether the legislature wishes to foster a policy of encouraging intoxicated drivers to pull off the road to sleep, includes considering the importance of the defendant's intent. Intent and policy an be looked at in two ways. The first, that presented by the Arizona court in *Zavala*, is that the driver who realizes that he is not in condition to drive and pulls off the roadway to sleep should be rewarded. If the court were not to reward such behavior, then the driver would be tempted to proceed to his destination and would present a greater threat to public safety. 136 Ariz. 356, 666 P.2d 456. The second view is that the drunken driver not only intended to drive but also did drive his car from the tavern to the freeway, and it is better policy to encourage an intoxicated person to avoid driving in the first place. In accord with this view, the Washington court noted that statutes prohibiting driving while intoxicated are primarily preventive measures that are designed to deter intoxicated persons from entering vehicles except as passengers. *Smelter*, 36 Wash. App. at 444, 674 P.2d at 693 (citing *State v. Ghylin*, 250 N.W.2d 252, 255 (N.D. 1977)). The *Smelter* court agreed with other courts that have held that such legislation should be liberally interpreted with the effect of promoting the public interest at the expense of the private interest of the inebriated driver. 36 Wash. App. at 444, 674 P.2d at 693.

Recent statutory revisions in Montana seem to follow this line of reasoning. The Montana legislature revised the traffic code in 1983 and purposely broadened the scope of the laws relating to drunken drivers. The intent was to allow patrol officers to apprehend drunken drivers before such drivers could create accidents. *Montana's Legislative Attempt to Deal with the Drinking Driver: The 1983 DWI Statutes*, 46 Mont. L. Rev. 315 (1985). The Montana court followed suit in *Taylor* by liberally construing the statutes. 242 Mont. 43, 661 P.2d 33. Considering the legislative intent and the court's demonstrated tendencies toward liberal construction, the court will probably side with Justice Ellett, who dissented in *Bugger:*

It does not matter whether the motor is running or is idle nor whether the drunk is in the front seat or in the back seat. His potentiality for harm is lessened but not obviated by a silent motor or a backseat position--provided, of course, that he is the one in control of the car. It only takes a flick of the wrist to start the motor or to engage the gears, and it requires only a moment of time to get under the wheel from the back seat. A drunk in control of a motor vehicle has such a propensity to cause harm that the statute intended to make it criminal for him to be in a position to do so. *State v. Bugger*, 25 Utah 2d 404, 405, 483 P.2d 442, 443 (1971) (Ellett, J., dissenting).

Conclusion

The Montana court will probably find that Andrew Renko was in actual physical control of a motor vehicle while intoxicated. Although it would be unprecedented to find "actual physical control" when the person was asleep across the front seat and the engine was not running, the Montana court has not been reluctant to break new ground. The court was a leader in defining "actual physical control," and many jurisdictions have followed the Montana definition.

Focusing on the threat to the public, the Montana legislature broadened the statutes to make it easier to apprehend intoxicated individuals before they cause motor vehicle accidents. The Montana court followed suit by broadly construing statutory wording. The tendency in Montana is toward an expanded definition. Therefore, it would be inconsistent for the court to conclude that Mr. Renko was not in actual physical control of his vehicle.

EXERCISE 22F: PARAGRAPH BLOCKS

This exercise should be done after reading Section 22.6 in the *Handbook*.

Mark the concluding paragraphs for paragraph blocks and the concluding sentences for individual paragraphs for the discussion section of the memo in Exercise 20E.

EXERCISE 22G: PARAGRAPH LENGTH

This exercise should be done after reading Section 22.6 in the *Handbook*.

Examine the length of the paragraphs on the memo in Exercise 20.E. Are any paragraphs too long? too short? Where would you add or take out paragraph breaks? Does the one-sentence paragraph ("In short, before the Montana court . . . ") work? If so, why? If not, why not?

Chapter 23
Connections Between Sentences

EXERCISE 23A: GENERIC TRANSITIONS

Each of the following pairs or sequences of sentences requires a generic transition to show the connection between the ideas. Select an appropriate generic transition and place it at the point of connection.

1. For ten years Mr. Hillary has owned a restaurant located on Puget Sound in Tacoma, Washington. Mr. Sam Wry owns the adjoining business, the Fitness Club, which has operated for one year. Mr. Hillary has become annoyed by the shop patrons wearing skimpy bathing suits during the aerobics class on the Fitness Club's lawn within full view of restaurant customers.

2. Wry has satisfied all necessary zoning and licensing requirements. He has legally opened the Fitness Club in the community.

3. Hillary will claim that the entire community is offended by the skimpy bathing suits and the loud raucous behavior at the Fitness Club. Hillary will claim that he is specially injured because he is losing the income from those patrons who will no longer eat at his restaurant.

4. In a 1964 opinion, the Court stated that just because "a thing is unsightly or offends the aesthetic sense of a neighbor does not ordinarily make it a nuisance or afford ground for injunctive relief." *Mathewson v. Primeau*, 64 Wash. 2d 929, 938, 395 P.2d 183, 189 (1964). The fact that some people were offended by activities at the Fitness Shop does not furnish a valid basis for a nuisance action.

5. The fundamental inquiry is whether the use of the property is reasonable or unreasonable. *Morin v. Johnson*, 49 Wash. 2d 275, 280, 300 P.2d 569, 571 (1956). The use must unreasonably interfere with another's use and enjoyment of property.

6. In *Turtle*, the court enjoined the establishment of a lakefront resort on the grounds that management would be unable to control the patrons, that the privacy of the neighboring residents would be disturbed, and that such a resort was alien to the character of the neighborhood. *Turtle v. Fitchett*, 156 Wash. 328, 287 P. 7 (1930). Hillary may argue that the Fitness Club has failed to control the aerobics classes, as evidenced by the noise, that the established sedate environment in the restaurant has been disrupted, and that the Fitness Club's activities are alien to the refined and tastefully commercial nature of the locale.

7. Washington courts do not determine nuisance by subjective values. The presence of nuisance is evaluated in objective terms.

8. If the elements are not met, the plaintiff could not maintain an action for public nuisance. He could consider a cause of action for private nuisance.

9. In finding that a public beach and camp are not a public nuisance, the court found these points compelling. The noise complained of was "ordinary." *Warner v. Hayes Inv. Corp.*, 13 Wn.2d 306, 311, 125 P.2d 262 (1942). It came from people behaving "in an orderly manner." *Id.* No intoxicants were sold or permitted on the beach. *Id.* at 313. The activities did not affect the rights of the entire neighborhood equally. *Id.*

10. In *Hayes*, the court found that neighbors suffered some occasional minor annoyance from the beach's patrons but that such annoyances were not extraordinary or unusual from a group of people gathered for recreation. The court found that the noise and activity were insufficient to support a cause of action for nuisance.

Exercise 23B: Dovetailing

Dovetailing is the overlap of language between two sentences that creates a bridge between those two sentences. Dovetails are often created by moving the connecting idea to the end of the first sentence and the beginning of the second sentence, repeating key words, using pronouns to refer back to nouns in an earlier sentence, and using "hook words" (this, that, these, such) and a summarizing noun.

Revise the following sentences by using the dovetailing technique.

1. An official of the Justice Department asked Conan to inform him of any activities of Congressman Lemming that might be politically embarrassing. The Justice Department offered him a reward.

2. Conan had no personal motive for his actions. He assisted the Justice Department in order to receive a reward.

3. Washington courts have held that the State can be liable for actions that are operational. Discretionary, planning, and design actions are not included.

4.   Operational acts are ministerial acts that are performed by agents in accordance with the criteria set up by the State. The agents do not exercise their own judgment.

5.   Mr. Pugh took financial log books from Mr. Snowadzki's private desk, copied them, and delivered them to the IRS. The IRS examined Mr. Snowadzki's tax returns, and he was subsequently tried and convicted on two counts of filing false tax returns.

Exercise 23C: Dovetailing

The following paragraphs are choppy. Revise using the dovetailing technique.

1.   On December 4, 2009, Mrs. Clive White, who was then five and a half months pregnant, was driving through an intersection when her car was struck by a car driven by seventeen-year-old Randy Thompson. Mrs. White was thrown against the dashboard and against the passenger side of the car. She gave birth to a stillborn child that same night. She is suffering severe emotional distress.

2.   A foreseeable risk, one that public officials knew of or should have known of, can be established through objective evidence. Injuries incurred by plaintiffs in similar situations would be an example. A jury would determine the foreseeability of the harm that the defendant had a duty to reasonably guard.

The following paragraph is somewhat disjointed because the writer violated the old --> new principle in spots. Revise accordingly.

3.   In October 2009, the Governor formed a panel of experts to study the daycare service crisis. Panel members visited daycare facilities throughout the state and wrote a report on their findings. The Governor, by Executive Order, initiated a daycare facility program inspection after conferring with panel members and considering their report. Pursuant to the order, the Secretary of the State Department of Social and Health Services studied the panel's report, developed a set of inspection criteria, and circulated the criteria via interdepartmental memorandum. The inspectors were directed by the memorandum to consider seven factors.

Chapter 24
Effective Sentences

This exercise should be done after reading Section 24.1.1 in the *Handbook.*

After labeling the subject of the sentence with "S" and the verb with "V" and the direct object with "O" (if there is an object), decide whether each sentence below is active or passive voice.

1. The plaintiff accepted the settlement offer.

2. Texas law requires a balancing of circumstances presented in each individual case.

3. This term will be arbitrarily defined by either a judge or jury.

4. In the absence of legislative direction, the court has reluctantly followed this trend.

5. The case for the defendant may be strengthened by considering the relative cost to the various parties.

6. The prescriptive easement had been established by the objective acts of the claimant.

7. The claimant's objective acts had established the prescriptive easement.

8. The Whalers' right to use the access road can be revoked by Mrs. Townsend.

9. Mrs. Townsend can revoke the Whalers' right to use the access road.

10.   Historically, interpretation of the rule has been left to the court's discretion.

EXERCISE 24B: PASSIVE VOICE

This exercise should be done after reading Section 24.1.2 in the *Handbook.*

The following sentences are all written in passive voice. In some cases even the dependent clauses (see Chap. 27.1) are in passive voice. Note how awkward passive voice makes many of these sentences. Rewrite the sentences in active voice and underline the verbs in both the main clauses and the subordinate clauses.

1.   Pearson & Sons Lawn Service is owned by Clyde Pearson.

2.   After Mr. Lee's truck was found in the ditch by Officer O'Neill, an ambulance was called for by Officer O'Neill.

3.   The idea that to prevent the dumping of toxic waste was intended by the legislature was focused on by the Montana court.

4.   Although the marijuana was not found in the bedroom by the police, a film canister filled with cocaine was found by Officer Miller.

5.   Important particularities are stipulated in the Fourth Amendment: the place to be searched and the things to be seized must be stated in the warrant.

6.   Fremont's argument that his right to privacy was violated by the broad scope of the search is supported by the *Anderson* court's language.

7.   Apparently, the business car had been driven by Tom on prior occasions, but specific permission to drive the business car was not given to him by his father on the day of the accident.

8.   The question of whether a non-viable fetus is a minor child has not been ruled on by the courts; however, the rights of non-viable fetuses in other areas of the law are recognized by the courts.

9.   The fair market value of the tractor should be recovered by the Wilsons because the recovery of the fair market value of property that has been destroyed is provided for by Washington tort law.

10.   A private nuisance is defined by statutory law as "everything not included as a public nuisance."

EXERCISE 24C: PASSIVE VOICE

The exercise should be done after reading Section 24.1.3 in the *Handbook*.

Read each of the following sentences and decide if the passive voice in the underlined section is used effectively or ineffectively. Write "E" for effective or "I" for ineffective, and then briefly explain why and, if necessary, in what context the passive voice is effective or ineffective.

1.   A lawful business <u>will not be enjoined</u> without a clear showing that it is impossible or impractical to eliminate its offensive features.

2.   In the past, Big Yard Toys Inc. would hire a subcontractor to install the equipment only if such arrangements <u>were requested</u> by the purchaser.

3. For the next ten years, the easement <u>was used</u> by all the landowners.

4. The plaintiff has testified that she <u>was assaulted</u> by a white male with blue eyes and blond hair. The defendant is a white male with brown eyes and black hair.

5. Testimony from the attending physician corroborates the victim's testimony that she <u>was struck</u> from behind.

6. Cathy's Creations is a designer clothing company <u>owned by</u> Cathy Nock. Ms. Nock employs a small staff to assist in the design and manufacture of the clothing.

7. Traditionally, if any element to a contract <u>has been omitted</u>, the contract is invalid.

8. Before the accidental poisoning, some of Mrs. Harris's medication <u>had been placed</u> in an old vitamin bottle.

9. A standard form contract that detailed the terms of the agreement <u>was signed</u> by both parties.

10. The Dead Man Statute <u>was intended</u> "to prevent the invasion of a deceased person's estate . . . ."

EXERCISE 24D: CONCRETE SUBJECTS

This exercise should be done after reading Section 24.2 in the *Handbook.*

Mark the subject and verb in the following sentences with an "S" and "V" and then revise the sentence to have a concrete subject. In some cases, you will have to create your own concrete subject.

1. It could be argued by the defense that Mr. Smith was out of the state at the time of the robbery.

2.	It is clear that both parties intended to enter into a contract.

3.	It is highly unlikely that a fair market value existed for the poem.

4.	Endorsement of the check is required before the funds can be transferred.

5.	It would appear that our request for punitive damages will be granted.

6.	Congressional confirmation is required for all federal judicial appointments.

7.	It is a known fact that the defendant was refused admission to medical school because of his criminal record.

8.	The aspect of the case that will be difficult to discount is Mr. Nolan's fingerprints on the knife.

9.	It should be pointed out that South Land Timber's shipments to all three customers were consistently late.

10.	The factor of the defendant's earlier perjury conviction caused the jury to discount her testimony in this case.

EXERCISE 24E: ACTION VERBS

This exercise should be done after reading Section 24.3 in the *Handbook.*

Mark the subject and verb in the following sentences with an "S" and "V" and then revise the sentence to have a more effective action verb. In sentences beginning with *there* the subject will follow the verb.

1. The way that a court determines mutual assent is to look at the objective manifestations of the parties' actions.

2. The governor made a statement that he would not testify for the defense.

3. The jury had knowledge of the defendant's prior record.

4. There are several facts that must be confirmed by that witness.

5. *Hanford v. Goehry* concerned a car that was kept at the father's place of business.

6. The nurse made an attempt to disconnect the life support system.

7. The *Harbeson* court made the suggestion that the Florida courts are moving towards awarding compensation for loss without applying the old standards.

8. There were no instances where the Parkers asserted their rights against the Lindquists.

9. *State v. Hughes* involved a defendant who shot two police officers while resisting arrest for another murder.

10. The two heirs are in disagreement over the division of property.

EXERCISE 24F: SUBJECT-VERB DISTANCE

This exercise should be done after reading Section 24.4 in the *Handbook.*

Mark the subject and verb with "S" and "V" and then revise the sentence so that the subject and verb are closer together.

1. A standard form contract that detailed all the terms of the agreement except for the shipper's liability was signed by both parties.

2. Goods that sell for over five hundred dollars ($500.00) must have the transaction in writing.

3. The possibility that an intoxicated driver may decide to continue driving rather than be arrested after pulling over to the shoulder of the road is what influenced the legislature to revise the statute.

4. Another theory available to Mr. Henderson but not to his co-defendants is the "moral right doctrine."

5. Lloyd's statement to his tax preparer that "the lunches were really social" indicates that Lloyd intentionally misrepresented at least some of the information.

6. The court's reading of the written contract, despite its insistence that there was no accompanying oral agreement, favored the tire manufacturer.

7. The court in another case involving the revision of a law manual stated that "the purchase of a copyright did not carry with it a license to defame . . . ."

8. Our client's name and reputation as a upstanding citizen and honest businessman who treats his employees fairly have been injured by the libelous conduct of *Trade Union World*.

9.   The concept of voluntary assumption of duty, when applied to the present case, suggests that the State voluntarily assumed a duty to use due care in conducting inspections of nursing homes.

10.   The state's argument that it owes a duty only to the public generally and not to any individual is not persuasive.

EXERCISE 24G: SUBJECT-VERB REVIEW

This exercise should be done after reading Section 24.4 in the *Handbook*.

In the following excerpt from a client letter, the ineffective subject/verb units have been underlined. First, decide why the subject/verb unit is ineffective (ineffective use of passive voice, weak subject, weak verb, too much distance between subject and verb) and then revise for an effective subject/verb unit.

Dear Ms. Garcia:

        My research on your claim against your ex-landlord, Joe Printer, for the return of
            1S
your damage deposit is complete, and I think you will be pleased with the results. The
                    1V
basis for my opinion is current statutory provisions and the following facts you related
2S   2V
during your visit to my office.

        On March 1, 2003, you entered into a valid written lease agreement. That

lease was terminated effective May 31, 2009, when you delivered a signed letter to Mr.
3S   3V
 Printer to that effect.

        This letter of notice of termination was received with at least 30 days' notice and
            4S   4V
was accepted as valid. As of September 10, 2009, you are without reimbursement of
4V   5S 5V
your $800.security deposit and you are without a written explanation from your former
                        5S 5V
landlord telling why he has not returned the money. Since the termination of your

lease, four letters to Mr. Printer inquiring about the deposit have been sent by you.
        6S   6V
Although you left a forwarding address, you have not received a reply. The apartment
                                            7S
was left clean and undamaged, except for normal wear and a small crack in the
7V

24-8

bedroom window.

The issue is whether under these circumstances you can force Mr. Printer to refund your $800.00 security deposit. An <u>examination</u> of the relevant Iowa statute
8S
currently in effect <u>reveals</u> that you have a strong chance of recovering your deposit.
8V

Generally, the <u>requirement</u> in the law for landlords <u>is</u> that within thirty days of
9S   9V
termination and receipt of the tenant's new address they must either return the damage deposit or provide the tenant with a written statement listing reasons for withholding the deposit. Since no <u>refund</u> or <u>statement</u> <u>was sent</u> by Mr. Printer, the law seems to
10S   10S   10V
support your claim.

EXERCISE 24H: SENTENCE LENGTH

This exercise should be done after reading Section 24.5.1 in the *Handbook*.

For each of the following overly long sentences, revise either by breaking the sentence into two or more shorter sentences or by using punctuation to create manageable units of meaning within the sentence.

1.   Traditionally, Florida courts have deferred to the legislature's policy judgment on the propriety of punitive damages awards and have manifested this deference by adhering rigidly to the rule that punitive damages should be awarded with the greatest caution and only where specifically authorized by statutes.

2.   The two critical factors the court will examine in determining whether a private citizen is an instrument or agent of the government are (1) the government's knowledge or acquiescence and (2) the intent of the party performing the search.

3.   Infringement is an interference with the rights granted to another under a law, a regulation, or a contract, and is usually categorized as infringement of copyrights, infringements of patents, or infringement of trademarks.

4. In *Board of Regents*, the court held that a jury instruction regarding arson was correctly withheld from the jury by the trial court because the theory of arson was only a mere possibility and did not rise above speculation and conjecture.

5. In *E.I. duPont de Nemorus & Co., Inc. v. Christopher*, the defendants used an airplane to photograph the plaintiff's Beaumont plant, which contained, in an open area, a secret but thus far unpatented process for producing methanol that had been developed by duPont at considerable time and expense and that provided duPont with a significant advantage over its competitors.

6. The insurance adjuster's testimony that the defendant's brakes were not functioning properly was based upon a physical inspection of the accident area for skid marks both the night of the accident and the next day during daylight where he found one distinct skid mark and one virtually non-existent skid mark.

7. *Question Presented*

    Under a negligence per se or a common law theory of negligence, is a tavern owner liable for serving alcohol to a minor without checking her identification and continuing to serve alcohol to her after she spilled a drink and sang while on top of a table, and later a personal injury car accident occurred when the car she was driving collided with another vehicle?

8. The plaintiff may obtain a summary of facts known and opinions held by the nontestifying expert through depositions of occupants of the cars or through another expert evaluating the facts and making his or her own conclusions.

9.   *Question Presented*

      Under N.Y. Penal Law § 125.25(3) (McKinney 1975), the felony murder rule, would a charge of second degree murder be valid for a defendant who was one of three participants in a robbery of a store owner with a previous heart condition who subsequently died of a massive heart attack that his physician states was undoubtedly caused by the stress of the robbery?

10. The felony-murder rule applies regardless of the victim's previous heart condition and the foreseeability of his death because robbery is inherently dangerous to human life and because a nexus has been established between the robbery and homicide.

EXERCISE 24I: SENTENCE LENGTH

This exercise should be done after reading Section 24.5.1 in the *Handbook.*

Read the following excerpt from the beginning of a discussion section for an office memo. Most of the sentences are too long. Revise by (a) breaking up a sentence into two or more separate sentences, (b) using punctuation breaks to create a manageable unit of meaning within a sentence, and (c) eliminating unnecessary wordiness.

Discussion

      In 1974, Congress voted on and then passed the Equal Credit Opportunity Act (hereinafter ECOA) in order to ensure that all financial institutions and all other firms engaged in or otherwise involved in the extension of credit make that credit equally available to all customers who are worthy of credit without regard to their sex or marital status. *Equal Credit Opportunity Act of Oct. 28, 1974*, Pub. L. No. 93-495, § 502, 88 Stat. 1521 (1974) (current version at 15 U.S.C. §§ 1691-1691(f) (1982). In 1976, Congress expanded the ECOA to prohibit credit discrimination based on race, color, national origin, age, receipt of public assistance income, or the exercise in good faith of the rights guaranteed under the Consumer Credit Protection Act. *Equal Credit*

Opportunity Act Amendments of 1976, Pub. L. No. 94-239, §§ 1-8, 90 Stat. 251 (1975) (current version at 15 U.S.C. §§ 1691-1691(f) (1982)).

The ECOA was enacted as a consumer protection statute designed to provide accurate information to and about customers involved in credit transactions and an antidiscrimination statute designed to shield protected classes of consumers from discrimination in the granting of credit. The Federal Reserve Board promulgated regulations to further those statutory goals. John H. Matheson, *The Equal Credit Opportunity Act: A Functional Failure*, 21 Harv. J. on Legis. 371 (1984).

EXERCISE 24J: SENTENCES REVIEW

This exercise should be done after reading Section 24.5.3 in the *Handbook*.

Read the following excerpts from a memorandum of points and authorities in opposition to motion for temporary custody (your client is Mr. Barker). Decide (1) if any of the sentences are overly long, (2) if there is sufficient variety in the sentence lengths, and (3) if short sentences have been used effectively. Revise accordingly.

1. Mr. Barker is a stable, loving father, who will provide a stimulating home environment for the Barkers' two children, George and Karen. However, the psychiatrist's report suggests that Mr. Barker may be compulsive. CP 37. This trait is not unusual for a highly successful businessman who now, because of that success, has more flexibility in his work schedule and will have even more time for his children. CP 41. Furthermore, the psychologist's report agrees that Mr. Barker has potential to be a sensitive, outgoing, yet stable parent.

2. Mrs. Barker's psychological stability, however, is far from certain. She has been diagnosed as having histrionic tendencies and as being mildly hysterical. Mrs. Barker's psychologist states that these disorders make her prone to alcohol and chemical dependency. Once, this dependency became so severe that Mrs. Barker required medical care to cope with her alcoholism.

This exercise should be done after reading Section 24.5.3 in the *Handbook.*

Read the following fact statement from the plaintiff's memorandum of law and authorities. Revise to improve sentence length by dividing overly long sentences, using short sentences for emphasis, and eliminating wordiness.

Lester and Marie Franklin, plaintiffs, (Franklins) operate a combination grocery store and delicatessen at 704 Filbert Street, San Francisco, California, on premises owned by Tyler and Tina Morgan (Morgans).

On September 22, 2009, the Franklins and Morgans entered into a lease agreement for the premises for eighteen (18) years with an option to terminate at the end of the (10) years. (See lease agreement attached as Exhibit A.) In essence, the lease provided for payment of base rent, percentage rent, taxes, and insurance and permitted the Franklins to perform tenant improvements as approved by the Morgans.

Additionally, under the lease (Ex. A Paragraph 5) the Franklins agreed to maintain and repair the premises, except for the roof, exterior walls and foundation, which were reserved to the Morgans and made their responsibility.

While the Franklins were making the pre-approved tenant improvements, the City of San Francisco performed an inspection and determined that the brick parapets, which are part of the exterior wall existing above the roof line, needed to have seismic bracing work performed. Without this bracing, the City would not grant the final permit to allow Franklin to open their business.

It is important to point out that the seismic bracing was not part of the tenant improvements prepared by the Franklins and approved by the Morgans. Further, the seismic bracing was not required because of the character of the Franklins' business and would have been required for any tenant, regardless of the business being conducted on the premises.

At the time the requirement for seismic bracing arose and was made mandatory by the City of San Francisco, the Morgans were unavailable, vacationing in Mexico. Consequently, they were not available to perform the repairs, although the lease provisions specifically reserved to the Morgans the responsibility for the exterior walls. Faced with the proposition of being unable to open their business and thereby incurring substantial damages and possibly increased costs to perform the repairs, the Franklins chose to advance and pay for the cost of the repairs and then recoup the cost from the Morgans, pursuant to the lease terms.

The Franklins immediately paid the construction and engineering costs and sought reimbursement from the Morgans, who refused payment, contending that the Franklins accepted the premises "as is" and further, that although the bracing was required on a part of the structure specifically reserved to the Morgans, the bracing did not constitute a repair.

At the time of the arbitration, the case sits in this posture: The Franklins are seeking recovery from the Morgans for the amount to repair the exterior wall, and the Morgans are seeking a judgment that they are not responsible for the repair cost.

EXERCISE 24L: EMPHASIS

This exercise should be done after reading Sections 24.6.1 - 24.6.4 in the *Handbook*.

Use the positions of emphasis and changes in punctuation to make the required revisions for emphasis.

Use sentence A for numbers 1 and 2:

(A)   The girl was tied to a tree and wearing only her shoes when the police officers found her.

    1. Revise sentence A to emphasize that the girl was tied to a tree.

    2. Revise sentence A to emphasize that the girl was wearing only shoes.

Use sentence B for number 3:

(B)   On July 14, 1986, a nuclear accident that killed seven people and that was the first fatal accident at the Nevada site occurred at Beatty, Nevada.

3. Revise sentence B to emphasize that seven people were killed and that this was the first fatal accident at this site.

Use sentence C for number 4:

(C)   A judge has the option of sentencing him to a period of two to ten years and imposing a fine not to exceed $5,000 if the defendant is convicted of this offense.

4. Revise sentence C to emphasize the possible jail term.

Use sentence D for number 5:

(D)   The plaintiff's final argument will depend on whether he can prove an over $20,000 depreciation of the value of his property.

5. Revise sentence D to emphasize the $20,000.

Use sentence E for numbers 6 and 7:

(E)   Under the Uniform Building Code, the tenant has no maintenance obligations; the owner is obliged to maintain the building.

6.   Revise sentence E to emphasize that it is the owner has the maintenance responsibility.

7.   Revise sentence E to emphasize that the tenant is not obligated to maintain the building.

Use sentence F for number 8:

(F)   The fact that the dog has bitten three people is our proof that he is vicious.

8. Revise sentence F to emphasize that the dog has bitten three people.

Use sentence G for numbers 9 and 10:

(G) The church freely admits that it did not have a special use permit when it operated a fulltime school.

9. Revise sentence G to emphasize that the church had no special use permit.

10. Revise sentence G to emphasize that the church makes the admission freely.

EXERCISE 24M: SINGLE WORD EMPHASIZERS

This exercise should be done after reading Section 24.6.5 in the *Handbook*.

Using the suggested single word emphasizer, revise the following sentences. Some restructuring of the sentence may be necessary.

1. Although five witnesses have placed Sharon Clark at the scene of the crime, she claims she was at home alone. (STILL)

2. An explosives expert testified that a slight change in the cabin pressure would activate the detonator. (ANY)

3. According to company regulations, an employee could not leave his or her post until the supervisor on duty had assigned a replacement. (NO)

4. In the union's history, an allegation of this severity has not been made. (NEVER)

5. It was the deceased who ran the stoplight. The defendant did not run the stoplight. (Revise into one sentence and use comma + NOT)

6. The bonds in the safety deposit box were under her name. (ALL)

7. The bonds in the safety deposit box were under her name. (ONLY)

8.   The members of the union voted to ratify the contract. (EVERY)

9.   Despite numerous warnings from the Environmental Protection Agency, National Chemical disposed of waste by-products by dumping them into the bay. (STILL)

10.   The operation did not cause Laura Smith's death. She died from inadequate post-operative care. (Revise into one sentence and use comma + NOT.)

EXERCISE 24N: CHANGING WORD ORDER

This exercise should be done after reading Section 24.6.6 in the *Handbook*.

Change the normal word order in the following sentences to emphasize the part that is underlined.

1.   The defendant was later identified <u>in a lineup with no other bearded men</u>.

2.   The defendant forced Ms. Harper to perform fellatio <u>at gunpoint</u>.

3.   Two witnesses have identified <u>the starter's pistol</u> as the weapon used.

4.   The trial court's exercise of this discretion will be overturned on appeal <u>only for a manifest abuse</u>.

5.   Mere assertions do not satisfy <u>the burden of proof</u>.

6.   The defendant could have effectively corrected all alleged errors <u>at the time they were made</u>.

7.   The State had strong evidence <u>on each separate count</u>.

8.   The definition of deadly weapon includes <u>the words "pistol"</u> <u>and "revolver."</u>

9.   The defendant's motion to sever Counts I and II from Counts III, IV, and V was <u>also denied</u>.

10. The defendant was convicted by the jury <u>on all five counts</u>.

EXERCISE 24O: BREAKING A PATTERN

This exercise should be done after reading Section 24.6.8 in the *Handbook.*

From each group of sentences, formulate one sentence or a sequence of sentences that uses a pattern. When appropriate, deliberately break the pattern for emphasis.

1.   There is a clear pattern in Mr. Baylor's behavior. He started by intimidating his children. His next victim of intimidation was his wife. Now he has been intimidating a witness.

2.   In October, Thomas Dever threatened Miss Stein. At the time he was not insane. He was also not insane when he shadowed her for two weeks in November and when, on Christmas Eve, he brutally killed her.

3.   We want to believe that our country acted fairly and wisely. It is hard for us to believe that it acted maliciously.

4.   After twenty years in prison, Carl Wilson returned to society. He did not have a job or a home. He had no money in the bank.

5. The opposition lacks proof that the defendant was at the scene of the crime. Furthermore, they cannot prove that he had a motive, much less that he committed the deed.

6. Neither a court nor a jury can undo what Frank Morris has done. Even a jail term will not undo what he has done.

7. Desmond Adams rebuilt his business with his own money. He did all the hard work, and he did not depend upon the help of his former partners.

8. Judith Davis, not her husband Martin, refused to see a marriage counselor. She was also the one who filed for divorce. Now she wants an even larger share of his pension.

9. Kyle Davis had a silent partner, Ronald Thomas, in the contract for the Lowell building and in the contract for the Madison complex. He acted alone in the contract for the Westside shopping mall.

10. With malice aforethought, Michael Mann bought a .38 caliber pistol at Seaside Pawn Shop and then waited in his car for Howard Peterson to return home from work and then followed him up to his front door and shot him three times in the chest.

EXERCISE 24P: EMPHASIS APPLICATION

This exercise should be done after reading § 24.6 in the *Handbook*.

Using a memo or brief that you have already written, check to see if you have used either of the two weaker strategies for emphasis: (1) telling the reader what is important or (2) underlining. Also check to see if you have used clearly, obviously, or very as single word emphasizers. Where appropriate, revise by omitting these strategies for emphasis or using another strategy for emphasis.

EXERCISE 24Q: EMPHASIS APPLICATION

This exercise should be done after reading § 24.6 in the *Handbook*.

Using a memo or brief that you have already written, check for the following strategies for emphasis. Revise where appropriate.

a.   short sentences
b.   positions of emphasis
c.   punctuation for emphasis
d.   single word emphasizers
e.   changes in normal word order
f.   repetition of key words
g.   patterns

Chapter 25
Effective Words

This exercise should be done after reading Sections 25.1.1 - 25.1.3 in the *Handbook*.

Find the inappropriate or imprecise word choice(s) in each of the following sentences. Write in the word(s) that you think expresses (express) the writer's intended meaning.

1.   All of these factors exhibit that it would be in the best interest for the children to modify the child custody agreement.

2.   The court will constitute this as an established custodial environment.

3.   This memorandum will display how this statute applies to Ms. Lynch's claim.

4.   The court may have psychological tests given to the kids.

5.   The *Gertz* court explored to find if Gertz had availed himself to the press.

6.   It is tough to know whether the court would award a partial injunction against the health club.

7.   Washington State courts have adopted the general and the limited public figure tests annunciated in *Gertz*.

8.   The corporation ceased in August 2008.

9.   The trial court decreed that the plaintiffs should be awarded damages and decreed a permanent injunction against keeping swine in excess of one boar, two brood sows, and their litters not over six months old.

10. The commission was set to oversee health care.

11. All these things must be proved beyond a preponderance of the evidence.

12. In *Yee v. Dept. of Environmental Services, Multnomah County*, 826 F.2d 877, 881 (1987), the court found that an American of Chinese dissent is a member of a class of persons protected on the basis of race.

13. When Duckworth tied the handkerchief around McCormack's jaw, he exasperated her condition by inhibiting her flow of oxygen.

14. Under the Federal Tort Claims Act, which evokes Washington law of *respondeat superior*, is the government liable for the negligent act of its employee when that employee, while traveling from a temporary base in California to his home base in Washington and while traveling in a rented car supplied by the government, subsequently hit a civilian's car when reentering the highway after he took a lunch break and a short sightseeing trip and caused extensive personal injuries to the civilian?

15. The plaintiff had arterial motives and timed her complaints to coincide with the date when the board would decide on her tenure application.

This exercise should be done after reading Section 25.1.4 in the *Handbook*.

Revise the following excerpt from a memo so that the writer uses the same term for the same idea.

A court will need to examine the tests for two doctrines, *respondeat superior* and "loaned servant," to determine whether Dr. Robinson or Bondurant Temporary Agency, Inc. (Bondurant) can be held vicariously liable for the destruction of Ms. Bakerman's coat. The first doctrine, *respondeat superior*, has a three-prong test. The first two prongs of the test are met. First, Carol Kester was negligent for the destruction of the coat. *See Nyman v. MacRae Bros. Constr. Co.*, 69 Wash. 2d 285, 287, 418 P.2d 253, 254 (1966). Second, Carol was acting within the scope of her employment at the time of the tortious act. *See Kuehn v. White*, 24 Wash. App. 274, 277, 600 P.2d 679, 682 (1979). There will, however, be a dispute about the third test: whether Carol was under the control of Bondurant, her general employer, or under the control of Dr. Robinson, her temporary employer at the time the coat was destroyed. *See Kroshus v. Koury*, 30 Wash. App. 258, 263, 633 P.2d 909, 911 (1981) (quoting *McLean v. St. Regis Paper Co.*, 6 Wash. App. 727, 732, 496 P.2d 571, 574 (1972)).

The second defense, "loaned servant," has a three-part test to determine who has control of a temporary employee. *Pichler v. Pacific Mechanical Constr.*, 1 Wash App. 447, 450-51, 462 P.2d 960, 963 (1969). The first and second parts of the test-- who has the right to select or hire and fire the servant and who has the right to direct how the servant shall perform his duties--will be disputed, but the most important test will be who had exclusive control or the right to exclusive control at the time of the tortious act. *Pichler*, 1 Wash. App. at 450-51, 462 P.2d at 963.

This exercise should be done after reading Section 25.1.6 in the *Handbook.*

Revise the following sentences and paragraphs so that the same term is used for the same idea and so that appropriate comparisons are being made (for example, comparing a case to another case is an appropriate comparison, comparing a defendant to a case is not.) If the sentence is already correct, simply mark it as correct.

1.   The grief over the loss of a six-week-old fetus is hardly comparable to a viable fetus.

2.   This policy of protecting the investor from the various schemes devised by promoters has been a persuasive cornerstone for judicial interpretation of investment contracts in the post-*Howey* era. *See, e.g., SEC v. Glenn W. Turner Enter., Inc.*, 474 F.2d 476 (9th Cir. 1973). However, the Ninth Circuit apparently does not find consumer protection alone determinative when interpreting federal securities law. Other factors may come into play, such as the underlying nature of the financial relationship between the buyer and the promoter. *See, e.g., Brodt v. Bache & Co., Inc.*, 595 F.2d 459 (9th Cir. 1978). Consequently, legal analysis of CP's money-making scheme does not yield a precise conclusion about whether a Ninth Circuit federal court would deem it to be an investment contract.

3.   The problem with comparing *Turner* to the present case is that the court offers no explanation about why the common enterprise prong was satisfied.

4. A potential plaintiff would argue that the fetus is the personal property of the mother. This argument would be similar to *Moore* in that the body part that was surgically removed was the personal property of the plaintiff patient.

5. In its decision, the *Brodt* court explicitly rejected using the concept of "horizontal commonality" employed in other circuits; that approach would require that there be a pooling of interests combined with a pro-rata sharing of profits. *Id.* at 460. Instead, the court used the broader principle of "vertical commonality," which requires that the investor and the promoter be involved in some common venture without mandating that other investors also be involved in the venture. *Id.* at 461 (citing *Hector v. Wiens*, 533 F.2d 429 (9th Cir. 1976)).

EXERCISE 25D: SUBJECT-VERB-OBJECT COMBINATIONS

This exercise should be done after reading Section 25.1.6 in the *Handbook.*

Isolate the subject, verb, and object and read them together to determine whether the subject/verb/object combinations in the following sentences make sense. When necessary, revise for precision. (The subject/verb/object mismatch may be in the main clause or in a subordinate clause.)

1. The language of the courts since then has broadened.

2. As for the burden of proof, *Eggert* says that the burden is on the plaintiff to establish a right to maintain the action in an action for conversion.

3. Should Mr. Robinson bring suit, the great weight of the case law would deny him relief.

4. A conviction under section 1071 in the Fourth Circuit has been interpreted as requiring proof of four elements: 1) that a federal warrant had been issued for the fugitive's arrest; 2) that the defendant had knowledge that a warrant had been issued for the fugitive's arrest; 3) that the defendant actually harbored or concealed the fugitive; and 4) that the defendant intended to prevent the fugitive's discovery or arrest.

5. There are, however, public policy issues that argue persuasively to restrict a woman's right to fetal tissue.

6. The test for whether a nuisance exists is determined by the use to which the property is put.

7. The likelihood that the court will determine that this is an established custodial environment is favorable.

8. The trust fund doctrine, which was created by the equity courts to protect creditors when an indebted corporation dissolved, withheld the corporation's property to be used to pay off debts.

9. Even though New Age Aerobics may not be causing safety hazards, increased traffic congestion, or unsightly buildings, the cumulative effects of its activities should be considered.

10. The probability that Mrs. Davis can meet this required standard of proof is unlikely.

EXERCISE 25E: GRAMMATICAL AMBIGUITIES

This exercise should be done after reading Section 25.1.7 in the *Handbook*.

Do exercises 26.L, 26.M, 26.N, and 26.O of the *Practice Book* on dangling and misplaced modifiers.

EXERCISE 25F: CONCISENESS

This exercise should be done after reading Section 25.2.1 - 25.2.5 in the *Handbook*.

Revise the following sentences for wordiness by creating strong subject-verb units and by editing out expletives and throat clearing expressions.

1. There are two defenses available to Acme.

2. It seems more likely than not that you are bound by the written agreement simply because you signed it.

3. In determining whether there was a sudden emergency, courts also take into consideration whether there was sufficient warning that should have alerted the driver to the imminent danger.

4.	The court will give Fed. R. Civ. P. 4(d)(1) a liberal construction.

5.	A court might have the inclination to follow the view that "in a highly mobile and affluent society, it is unrealistic to interpret 4(d)(1) so that the person to be served has only one dwelling house or usual place of abode at which process may be left." 4A Charles Alan Wright & Arthur R. Miller, *Federal Practice and Procedures* § 1096, (2d ed. 1987).

6.	There is a difference in opinion between the two parties over whether the deposit is refundable.

7.	The court used the inference that because the papers were left with appellant's mother, the appellant received them.

8.	It appears that if "substantial" is held to be analogous with "principal," then five percent of a total business would be the minimum necessary to establish that certain sales of merchandise are a "principal" part of a business.

9.	An argument could be made that Ms. Fox so conditioned her acceptance of your offer as to create a counteroffer.

10.	It was the legislature's intention to encourage corporations to explore new ways of reducing energy costs.

11. After thoroughly researching your complaint against Mr. Brown, I have come to the conclusion that the best way to recover the $2,500 that he owes you is to file a lien against his orchard.

12. An important consideration to be kept in mind, however, is that the boys deny making any threats.

13. The defendant has made a motion to suppress the evidence seized after the arrest.

14. It was not error for the trial court to fail to instruct on the absence of intervening cause.

15. Subsequent to the court's overruling of the objection interposed by defense counsel, the witness answered in the affirmative.

This exercise should be done after reading Sections 25.2.6 - 25.2.8 in the *Handbook*.

Revise and edit the following sentences for pompous language, doubling phrases, needless repetition, and clutter.

1. Before I can begin advising you about the various aspects of your case, I need to ask the following question about whether or not your husband knew or was aware that his life expectancy was very short.

2. Furthermore, in addition to the procedure that is utilized to initiate the process, the foreman of the plant must initiate the contingency or back-up system at that same point in time.

3. It is the night watchman's usual custom to terminate his rounds at 5 a.m. in the morning after carefully performing an inspection of each and every safe in the building.

4. Obviously, prior to trial, the defendant will move by filing a Motion in Limine to exclude all of the evidence of his previous prior convictions.

5. The nature of the consensus of opinion among board members was that to implement a certain procedure that would be used by each and every employee when entering or leaving the building would not terminate the problems and difficulties the company was experiencing from employee theft.

6. It was believed and assumed by the Parkers that in situations where real estate agents list a home for sale, the real estate agents have an obligation and responsibility to appraise and determine the value of the home that is being listed.

7. For a period of two months during the year of 2009, Mr. Wilson aided and abetted a known felon by allowing her to utilize his cabin as a place to hide from law enforcement officers who were looking for her.

8. At the present time, there is clearly no constitutionally protected right to receive credit, but however there is a great deal that can be done to guarantee and insure that credit is available to all people on a just and fair basis.

9. In my own personal opinion, we cannot get an injunction from a court that will completely eliminate the use of the factory's noon whistle at 12:00 each day.

10. Our principal and basic policy objective in promulgating the order to vacate the premises of the building was to insure and otherwise guarantee that all of the inhabitants and residents of said premises were safe and secure.

This exercise should be done after reading Section 25.2.9 in the *Handbook.*

Edit the following sentences by reducing sentences to clauses, clauses to phrases, and phrases to words.

1.   In late October 1997, Kyle Nelson asked Frances Miles to house sit for him while he was away on vacation.   Frances Miles is an acquaintance of Kyle Nelson.

2.   The trial judge calculated O'Hara's offender score as seven.   She based her decision on Or. Rev. Stat. 137.370 (4).   That statute states in part that "[u]nless the court expressly orders otherwise, a term of imprisonment shall be concurrent with the remainder of any sentence previously imposed at the time the court imposes sentence."

3.   Instruction 10 did not shift the ultimate burden of proof to Chin.   Instruction 10 did not create any mandatory presumption.   It did not impose any burden of producing evidence on Chin.   Rather, the instruction states that the presumption "is not binding" upon the jury.   It further states that the jury can determine "what weight, if any," to give to the presumption.

4.   At the disposition hearing, the state presented a document describing Ortega's prior criminal history.   Ortega's prior criminal history consisted of ten burglary convictions and three minor offenses subject to diversion.

5. Peters moved to Chesterville to be near her husband. Her husband was an inmate at the state penitentiary at Chesterville. Upon arriving in Chesterville, Peters met a woman. The woman's husband was also an inmate in the penitentiary.

6. The legislature directed the Department of Ecology to publish a statutorily prescribed notice by four different means. These four different means are as follows: 1) publication of the notice once a year for five years in major as well as local newspapers; 2) publication of the notice every six months on radio and television stations broadcasting in every county; and 3) posting the notice in a conspicuous location in every county; and 4) including a copy of the notice with notices of taxes due for 1972 mailed by each county treasurer.

7. The Court of Appeals upheld the rape conviction and corresponding habitual criminal finding. However, the Court of Appeals reversed the assault conviction.

8. At 2:20 a.m. on September 29, 2008, Brian Smith entered his parents' bedroom. His parents were sleeping there at the time. Brian shot his mother in the head with a 30.06 rifle. This shot killed his mother. Mr. Smith woke up. He saw Brian leave the bedroom. He was unable to telephone for help because Brian had taken the telephone off the hook in the kitchen. Mr. Smith locked the bedroom door. He escaped through the window. Brian returned to the bedroom. He intended to kill his father. He found that his father had escaped.

9.   After the police arrived at the scene, the officers discovered Barbara Wilson-Hughes in a comatose condition. They immediately called an emergency medical unit. The emergency medical unit transported Mrs. Wilson-Hughes to a local hospital. At the hospital, she was treated for a "closed-head injury" and several facial lacerations.

10.   In *Workman*, the court set forth and applied a two-prong test for restricting and otherwise determining when lesser offense instructions should be given to the jury to use in its deliberations. The first prong of the test is that each of the elements of the lesser offense must be a necessary element of the offense charged. The second prong of the test is that evidence must support an inference that the lesser crime was committed.

EXERCISE 25I: CONCISENESS REVIEW

This exercise should be done after reading Section 25.2 in the *Handbook*.

Using all the strategies for concise writing in this section, revise and edit the following sentences for wordiness.

1.   Damages in the amount of $20,000 were paid to each plaintiff.

2.   Clearly, a driver of a motor vehicle who basically refuses to wear the glasses prescribed for him by his doctor and who continues to operate his vehicle at a rate of speed that exceeds the speed limit is an extremely dangerous hazard on the road.

3.   Testimony was elicited from Trooper Evans. Trooper Evans investigated the accident. Trooper Evans testified that the "primary casual factor" of the accident had been the defendant's intoxicated state.

4.   Apparently, there are two arguments Jones will make in his own defense. Jones will first make the argument that, prior to the search, he did not knowingly, willingly, and voluntarily give Officer Nguyen his consent to a search of his wallet. Jones will then make a second argument that the items that Nguyen discovered during the course of the search, most particularly the stolen charge card, exceeded and otherwise went beyond the scope of the consent that Jones gave to Officer Nguyen.

5.   Henson responded to the public disclosure request by providing all of the documents, except two letters. These two letters were excluded because of the fact that both of these letters contained proprietary or private information with regard to the business practices of Henson.

6.   For the most part, each of their mail was sent to each of their separate addresses, but sometimes, on occasion, an invitation would come to the address of Mr. Patel, and both of their names would be present on the invitation.

7.   Basically, Mr. McRae stated in a formal statement that he discussed only the manufacture and delivery of the equipment with Jim Drane. Jim Drane is the

principal of Lakeland Elementary. Mr. McRae reiterated over again that they did not discuss the matter of installation.

8. Based on a recognition of the fact that in cases very similar to yours in their facts the courts invariably issued a directed verdict, I am of the opinion that we can, with all probability, hope for and expect that you too will be granted a directed verdict in your case.

9. For all intents and purposes, the court was absolutely correct when it issued a denial of defendant's motion for a new trial for the very specific reason that the defendant must do more than merely suggest a "possibility of prejudice" when he moves for a new trial.

10. Due to the fact that my client was absolutely unaware of and uninformed about the state and federal law governing this matter and due to her advanced age and years, she should be considered for and granted special consideration by this court. Her primary and only desire was and is to give and bequeath her most prized and valuable collection of hand-painted china to the library of the community in which she has lived and resided during these past eighty-seven years.

This exercise should be done after reading § 25.2 in the *Handbook*.

Revise and edit the following paragraphs for wordiness.

1. As established in *Park v. Stolzheise*, 24 Wash. 2d 781, 167 P.2d 412 (1946), "comfortable enjoyment means both mental quiet and physical comfort." With regard to this definition, the neighbors will obviously argue that the floodlights being on until 12 midnight adversely affects their physical comfort in that their sleep is greatly disturbed by the bright lights beaming through the bedroom windows of the houses. To support this contention, the neighbors will further argue the *Bruskland* case where the court stated that headlights of an automobile that shined upon a bedroom window of a dwelling house unreasonably and substantially interfered with the comfort and enjoyment of the owners' property, thus constituting a private nuisance. 42 Wash.2d at 348. Consequently, therefore, it can be stated that the trial court or trial judge or jury would probably rule that the comfortable enjoyment of the neighbors of their property was interfered with by the shining of the floodlights.

2. Besides determining whether there was a pre-existing controversy, the court must also determine whether the plaintiff "thrust into the controversy in an attempt to influence the outcome." *Hutchinson*, 443 U.S. at 135. An example of thrusting into a controversy in an attempt to influence the outcome of the issues is found in *Waldbaum*. In *Waldbaum*, a controversy was developing in the supermarket industry. People were debating about the introduction of unit pricing and open dating into supermarkets. The plaintiff in *Waldbaum* purposefully attempted to influence the outcome of this public debate by holding a special meeting to which it invited both the press and the public.

3.   Although the two levels of immunity have been basically well defined, the level of immunity that parole board members should be afforded remains unclear and uncertain. In order to effectively analyze the case at hand, the court must assess the rules and tests of the jurisdictions governing this case. The court must examine the decisions of the Supreme Court, Third Circuit, and Ninth Circuit in regard to the levels of immunity accorded to public officials which will present the basic tests to determine the type and scope of immunity that the Board members should be afforded.

EXERCISE 25K: LEGALESE

This exercise should be done after reading Section 25.3 in the *Handbook*.

Read the following opinion letter and eliminate the legalese.

Dear Mr. Patterson:

Enclosed herewithin is a copy of the Notice of Appeal that was filed with the King County Superior Court on November 25. Said notice will be transferred to the Court of Appeals forthwith.

Because the case involves an issue of constitutional magnitude, it will be reviewed de novo. Nonetheless, prevailing on appeal is unlikely and improbable. As previously discussed, show-ups are not per se impermissible. Hence of the Court of Appeals will need, iteralia, to balance suggestiveness against the reliability of the identifications. To wit, appellate court will consider the five factors seriatum and probably reach the same conclusion as previously reached by trial court.

In spite of the fact that these cases are infrequently and rarely reversed on appeal, the utmost effort and diligence will be exercised on your behalf by all those in our firm. If all else fails, a writ of certiori will be filed with the Supreme Court on your behalf if you so request.

Very truly yours,

Ms. Sarah Fisher

EXERCISE 25L: GENDER-NEUTRAL LANGUAGE

This exercise should be done after reading Section 25.4 in the *Handbook*.

Substitute gender neutral language for the following phrases and sentences.

1. masked gunman

2. neighbor's wife (both husband and wife live together)

3. the family of man

4. Dear Board of Governors and Governesses

5. the woman driver in the second vehicle

EXERCISE 25M: GENDER-NEUTRAL LANGUAGE

This exercise should be done after reading § 25.4 in the *Handbook*.

Revise the following sentences by substituting gender neutral language for sexist language.

1. The operator of the vehicle left the scene without identifying himself.

2. When determining the status of a child as Indian, the state court must seek verification of his status from either the Bureau of Indian Affairs or from his tribe.

3. Evidence of the defendant's other offenses may not be admitted as proof of the charged offense if the evidence is relevant only to show his criminal disposition.

4. A guardian is a man lawfully invested with the power, and charged with the duty, of taking care of another who, for defect of age, understanding, or self-control, is considered unable to administer his own affairs.

5. Summary judgment should be denied if the moving party does not sustain his initial burden of proof and if reasonable men would reach different conclusions from the evidence presented.

6. When requesting that a judgment be set aside, the moving party's attorney must comply with CR 60(e)(1), which requires that he prepare an affidavit setting forth the facts constituting a defense.

7. The statute gives men and their wives more freedom to independently dispose of their property by contract, free from court supervision.

8. Mrs. Edwards is a working mother who has little time or energy left for her children at the end of the day. Mr. Edwards, on the other hand, operates his accounting business out of his home. Consequently, he is able to give the children the mothering they need.

9.   The Acme Loan Service informed Mr. Valdez and his wife that the liens would
      have to be removed before they could secure a loan.

10.   "It is the purpose of this subchapter to assure a meaningful disclosure of credit
      terms so that the consumer will be able to compare more readily the various
      credit terms available to him and avoid the uninformed use of credit, and to
      protect the consumer against inaccurate and unfair credit billing and credit card
      practices." 15 U.S.C. § 1601 (a).

11.   Rule 9 of the Admission to Practice Rules provides that a qualified law student,
      law clerk, or law school graduate may be granted a limited license to practice law
      if he 1) has completed at least two-thirds of a three-year course of studies, 2)
      has the written approval of his law school dean, and 3) has certified that he has
      read and is familiar with the Rules of Professional Conduct.

12.   Miss Helene Russell was a lady pharmacist in Baton Rouge, Louisiana, when a
      federal grand jury indicted her on fifteen counts of violating Title 21 U.S.C. §§
      841(a)(1), 841(b)(2), 843(a)(4), and 827(a)(3).

13.   The comment to subsection (a) of § 158 explains that a man may invade another
      man's property by "throwing, propelling, or placing a thing" either on the land or
      in the air above it.

14.   The airline's spokesman claimed that no man could have prevented the tragedy
      and that the accident was "an act of God."

15.   The court may impose an exceptional sentence for the offense of indecent liberties when the victim is particularly vulnerable or unable to resist because of her young age and when the offender shows that he is not amenable to treatment.

EXERCISE 25N: GENDER-NEUTRAL LANGUAGE

This exercise should be done after reading Section 25.4 in the *Handbook*.

Revise the following paragraph for sexist language.

1. The incident giving rise to the attempted rape charge occurred on November 1, 2009, when the defendant, Harold Strickland, went out on a date with Connie Osburn. About 12:30 a.m., Strickland drove Connie back to his apartment. Once inside, Strickland immediately forced Connie into the bedroom and onto the bed. Without her consent, he lay on top of her and tried to force his hand under her clothing. Connie then convinced Strickland that she needed to use the bathroom. He relented and, while she was in the bathroom, Connie escaped through a window. After finding a policewoman, Connie took her to the scene and showed her Strickland's apartment.

Chapter 26
Eloquence

There are no exercises for this chapter.

Chapter 27
Grammar

27A: FRAGMENTS

This exercise should be done after reading Section 27.2 in the *Handbook.*

Read the following and decide if they are complete sentences or fragments. If they are fragments, revise to make complete sentences.

1.   The defendant's story will not be told. If the court allows the prior convictions to be admitted into evidence.

2.   Mr. Barnett won a Pulitzer prize. Which generally gives a person worldwide recognition for his or her work.

3.   When an artist and author like Michael Barnett creates a prize-winning musical, he has two interests in the end product. The first interest is an economic one.

4.   The second interest, honor and reputation. "[T]he author wants to ensure that his creative   personality, expressed in his work, is preserved." Robert E. Hathaway II, *American Law Analogues to the Paternity Element of the Doctrine of Moral Right: Is the Creative Artist in America Really Protected?* 30 Copyright L. Symp. 121, 122 (1976).

5. Both of these crimes are considered violent crimes. Therefore, probably not of probative value to the state's case.

6. Although a technical case can be made for non-compliance with Rule 4(d)(1), the question of the overall efficiency of this approach is open to doubt. Especially in the light of potential service in New York under the California long arm statute.

7. The trend in American courts to balance economic and moral interests in the areas of contract and tort law. In European countries, the opposite is true.

8. The court has only one real issue to decide. Whether the Los Angeles home is the dwelling house of the defendant.

9. Unfair competition, a general term, embracing the narrower area of trademark law, which concerns the same legal wrong, namely, misrepresentations as to the source of goods or services.

10. The defendant states that Ms. Patten gave the coins to him as a gift. Whereas Ms. Patten alleges that she was robbed.

EXERCISE 27B: FRAGMENTS

This exercise should be done after reading Section 27.2 in the *Handbook.*

Read the following statement of facts from an office memo. Find and revise all sentence fragments.

Agnes and Arthur Hoffelmeir were on vacation between October 11 and October 20, 2009. Their neighbors, the Burgesses, offered to take care of their pet cat. Which the Hoffelmeirs were emotionally attached to and considered a member of the family.

On October 19, 2009, the cat went into Mrs. Kravitz's rose garden and began chewing the rose bushes. Although Mrs. Kravitz tried to shoo the cat away. The cat kept returning to the Kravitz yard to chew on the rose bushes. Because this had happened on several other occasions, Mrs. Kravitz called the Humane Society.

The Humane Society impounded the cat, and Mr. Janske of the Society tried unsuccessfully to contact the Hoffelmeirs. The cat was destroyed on October 20, 2009. Within 36 hours after impoundment and despite a city ordinance that states that an impounded dog must be held for at least 72 hours before it can be destroyed.

EXERCISE 27C: FRAGMENTS REVIEW

This exercise should be done after reading Section 27.2 in the *Handbook.*

Read the following excerpt from the same memo about the destruction of a pet cat. Find and revise all fragments that are not permissible uses.

In *Sequin*, a federal customs official impounded the plaintiff's car and failed to release her car in a timely manner. The court held that if the defendant's conduct could be interpreted as willful or malicious, the plaintiff could recover damages for emotional distress. *Id.* at 811.

We could argue that the Humane Society and Mr. Janske acted unlawfully. If they both were bound by the Sequin City Ordinance. And because the cat was destroyed before the time provided by the ordinance.

The Humane Society and Mr. Janske may make the following arguments. First, that *Sequin* refers to the unlawful garnishment or seizure of property, not the destruction of it. Second, that they acted within their legal duty when the cat was seized. Third, because they did not intentionally violate the city ordinance, their actions were not willful or malicious. Also because Mr. Janske attempted to contact the Hoffelmeirs before the cat was destroyed.

The Hoffelmeirs could counter these claims with the following arguments. First, the seizure of the cat may have been lawful. The destruction was not. While *Sequin* is concerned with the unlawful seizure of property, the unlawful destruction of property is even more serious. Therefore, the principle of *Sequin* should apply in this case.

Second, the destruction of the cat before the proscribed time period is malicious and willful misconduct. The Society and Mr. Janske being aware that pets are valuable to their owners. Mr. Janske should have waited until the Hoffelmeirs were contacted before the cat was destroyed. The city ordinance's requirement for a holding period so that pet owners will have an opportunity to claim their pets. If the Humane Society had abided by the ordinance, the cat would have been claimed, and the Hoffelmeirs would not have suffered this loss.

Third, given that the rationale against awarding punitive damages is that an injured party will be adequately compensated through other measures. And given that the replacement cost of the cat is not adequate compensation. The only way the Hoffelmeirs will receive adequate compensation is through an award of damages that includes compensation for mental anguish.

Finally, that there is persuasive authority to support the Hoffelmeirs' argument for damages for mental anguish. In a Louisiana case, a neighbor trapped the plaintiff's pet cat and brought it to the animal control center where the cat was destroyed. The plaintiffs sued to recover damages for the mental anguish and humiliation they suffered from the loss of their cat. The court held that they could be compensated for their mental anguish. If the plaintiffs suffered actual damages. *Peloquin v. Calcasier Parish Police Jury*, 367 So.2d 1246, 1251 (La. App. 1979).

EXERCISE 27D: VERB TENSE

This exercise should be done after reading Section 27.3.1 in the *Handbook*.

Read the following sentences and, where necessary, correct the tense of the verbs.

1.   The issue in *Farny* is whether the New Jersey address is the defendant's dwelling house or usual place of abode.

2.   In *Farny*, the plaintiff contends that the New Jersey address continues to be defendant's dwelling house or usual place of abode.

3.   Under Article III of the Constitution, the jurisdiction of federal courts is limited to cases and controversies. U.S. Const. art. III, § 1.

4.   In *Wagner*, the court held that the showup procedure was permissible, even though the police had asked the witness to identify a handcuffed suspect.

5.   In *Kraus*, the court held that the show up was not impermissibly suggestive when the victim of an attempted robbery was asked to identify the suspect after the police brought the suspect to the victim's place of business and when the police conducted a pat-down search of the suspect in front of the victim.

6.   Cases in the entertainment industry usually involve a misappropriation or
      attribution of one's name for economic gain.

7.   In *Bishop*, the court analyzed the predecessor to the current assault statute and
      concluded that aiming or discharging a firearm was not a lesser included offense
      of second degree assault.

8.   The State's evidence reveals that Michael informed the group that he had beaten
      McIvar.

9.   This court held that the *Edwards* construction must be read into the court rule as
      if that construction had been originally written into the rule.

10.   Officer Thompson arrived at the scene of an accident in which a car towing a
      small trailer went over an embankment.

EXERCISE 27E: VERB TENSE

This exercise should be done after reading Section 27.3.1 in the *Handbook*.

Read the following paragraphs and, where necessary, correct the tense of the verbs.

In 1976, Bob Rhumb built the Cummings's house. In May 1977, Rhumb builds a
garage and fence, and John Miller buys the lot north of Rhumb's lot--the lot that is now
Walker's--and builds a house on it that was completed toward the end of 1977. When
Rhumb finished building his garage and fence, he had planted his lawn, which extends

along a line from the fence to the street. Rhumb did not plant the three-foot strip that is now in dispute.

In the spring of 1978, Miller plants that strip with grass after Rhumb agreed to pay for a portion of the costs. In addition, along the back portion of his property, Miller plants a garden that extends onto the three-foot strip. From the time that Miller planted the lawn and garden in 1978 up to the present, he and the subsequent owners maintain the garden and mow the grass on the strip that is now in dispute.

During the time that he had owned the property, Rhumb never discusses the true boundary line with anyone, except for references to it on two occasions: once, in 1978, when he agreed with Miller to pay a portion of the grass seed costs, and again in 1993, during Kaiser's ownership, when Kaiser was out washing his car, he said something to Rhumb like "Hey, you oughta come over and wash my car 'cause I always mow your lawn."

In January 1998, the Kaisers sold the property to the Hemstads. The Hemstads live there until 2002 and then rent the house from 2002 until 2005, when they sell it to Debbie Walker. Walker and her predecessors have all maintained the garden and mowed the lawn just as the Millers did.

In 2009, our client, Charlie Cummings and his wife Anna buy the house previously occupied by Bob Rhumb. Cummings wants to remodel the house and replace the original garage, but the structure will be located about three feet north of the existing garage and fence. Debbie Walker has protested that the new structures, as described by our client, will be partially built on her property. Cummings has pointed out that the real property line had been located three feet north of the existing garage and fence, but Debbie Walker is attempting to obtain title by claiming adverse possession.

EXERCISE 27F: SUBJECT-VERB AGREEMENT

This exercise should be done after reading Section 27.4.1 in the *Handbook*.

Choose the form of the verb that agrees with the subject.

1.   All of the justices (was/were) in favor of reviewing the case.

2.   There (was/were) no further unexecuted acts to be performed by the landlord.

3.   Ms. Hernandez, as well as the two other employees, (has/have) testified that the alarm was never set.

4.   Not at issue in this case (is/are) those parts of Section 16-6-2 criminalizing sodomy by force.

5.   A majority of the panel (has/have) found that Montoya possessed sufficient standing to pursue the action.

6.   All of the evidence in this case (is/are) circumstantial.

7.   The Respondent, in seeking declaratory and injunctive relief, (claims/claim) that the statute violates his right to privacy under the First, Third, Fourth, Fifth, Ninth, and Fourteenth Amendments to the United States Constitution.

8.   Your problem (is/are) seven employees who want a cost of living adjustment added to their retirement benefits.

9.   "Known and unknown, foreseen and unforeseen bodily and personal injuries" (was/were) added to the updated version of the medical release form.

10.   The appellate court, in exceptional circumstances and as an exception to the rule, (considers/consider) questions not presented to the trial court if they involve a possible denial of due process or if criminal penalties attach.

11.   The injuries that Sullivan discovered after she had signed the release (raises/raise) a material issue of fact concerning the validity of the release.

12.   Reversing the summary judgment and remanding the case for trial (is/are) the only proper course of action the court can take.

13.   The *Finch* case, as well as the *Nellington* case, (is/are) distinguishable from Chang's situation.

14.   Each nurse and orderly at the station (was/were) in frequent contact with the patients in that wing.

15.   Neither the driver nor any of the passengers on the bus (has/have) admitted that the bus veered over the double yellow line.

16.   The procedures governing relief from a default judgment (is/are) set forth in CR 60, which allows the court to excuse a party from a judgment for, among other reasons, "mistakes, inadvertence, surprise, excusable neglect or irregularity in obtaining a judgment order." CR 60(b)(1).

17.   An affidavit from Grayson's attorney setting forth the procedural history of the case, along with excerpts from depositions of Crowell's supervisors and from Crowell himself, (has/have) been filed in support of the motion.

18.   A search of Abuya's car turned up a copy of "World Warriors," which (publishes/publish) articles glorifying the violent lives of mercenary soldiers.

19.   "Prior unrelated matters" (refer/refers) here to prior convictions.

20.   Every door and window to the victim's home (was/were) left unlocked.

This exercise should be done after reading Section 27.4.2 in the *Handbook*.
Read the following sentences and correct the errors in pronoun agreement. If the sentence has no pronoun agreement errors, mark it "correct."

1.   The appellate court upheld the trial court's verdict, stating that they found no manifest abuse of discretion.

2.   Under cross-examination, a witness may suddenly realize that their earlier testimony was inaccurate.

3.   Someone who makes an obscene telephone call is unlikely to use his real name.

4.   Courts interpreting the ECOA's actual damage provision have declared that a successful plaintiff may recover for injury to their credit rating, as well as damages for embarrassment, humiliation, and emotional distress.

5.   When a tax consultant prepares a tax return for a client, they use only what the client gives them.

6.   The police had reason to believe that either Collins or his companions were armed and dangerous based on their alleged involvement in the Bleauville robbery.

7.   The board firmly believed that their main responsibility was to protect Acme Textiles, Inc. from a hostile corporate takeover.

8.   Somebody used their master key to enter the storage room and remove the typewriter.

9.   The parents and their daughter have their hands bound behind their backs.

10.   In *Snowadzki*, the IRS successfully argued that they had nothing to do with where or how the records were going to be obtained.

11. In order to assert the sudden emergency doctrine, the party claiming the defense must   show that he or she is confronted by a sudden, unexpected peril, through no negligence of their own.

12. Harrison Tractor Company can argue that they were operating in good faith when they signed the agreement.

13. The store detective assumed that either the defendant or her mother must have hidden the bracelet in her purse.

14. When the trial court refused to submit the statutory instruction, it forced the jury to determine their own meaning for the terms "knowingly" and "interest," which may or may not have matched those established by the legislature.

15. The defendant, Jeffrey Lyons, argued that the trial court had no authority to impose a polygraph examination as a condition of his probation because they are unreliable.

16. Everyone living in the apartment complex parks their car in   the vacant lot across the street.

17. Neither his team nor his friend is willing to testify about Michael's threats to harm Principal Evans because they believe that those statements were "the drugs, not Michael, talking."

18. Only after the court has concluded that the evidence is relevant can they balance the probative value against the prejudicial effect.

19. The police report states that the unknown perpetrator of the crime removed a screen and left his fingerprints on the window.

20. The Water Rights Registration Act, Wash. Rev. Code § 90.14 (1989), which required every person who claimed water rights not evidenced by the 1917 or 1945 water codes to register their claim with the State before June 30, 1974, was updated in 1997 when the governor opened up the claims registry again.

This exercise should be done after reading Section 27.5.1 in the *Handbook.*

Revise the following sentences to clarify the ambiguous pronouns.

1. Howard Davis claims that the apartment manager yelled "Stop!", but he never made an effort to interfere.

2. Davidson cooperated in the search by telling the police about the money and plane ticket under the false bottom of his suitcase. Davidson asserts that it was from a recent trip to California.

3. Two brothers, Earl and Mason Hargrove, own two lumber yards, Eastside Building Supplies and Hargrove Lumber and Hardware. They are both financially stable.

4. O'Brien jammed the coins back behind the car seat and then hid the guns under the spare tire. After a complete search of the vehicle, they were found by Officer Martinez.

5. Juror Marc Stein stated to all other jurors that he had discussed the accident with his brother-in-law, a professional truck driver. He said that the accident could not have occurred as the defendant testified.

6. After giving chase, Officer Conner apprehended Helman, who had a red bandanna scarf wrapped around his hand. It had some glass fragments in it.

7. A claim by Stravinski that he was not present at the scene of the crime is not necessarily antagonistic with a claim by McDonald that he was present but did not commit the crime.

8.   After conducting a pat-down search of the defendant, Deputy Peterson found a razor blade wrapped in a tissue under his vehicle.

9.   Edna Lino testified that several men, including James Crowell, approached the petitioner after he slapped her. She further testified that he appeared to be afraid that he would beat him up.

10.   Clyde Reeves and his son, Daryl, were both injured in two automobile accidents that occurred within two months of each other. The first accident occurred on October 8, 2008, when he was injured in a rear end collision with a vehicle driven by Melvin Maye. He immediately sought and received medical care for the injuries from Dr. Charles Santino, his family physician. Later, on November 10, 2008, while still under his care, he was involved in an accident with a vehicle driven by Carter Szabo. He again sought and received medical treatment from him.

EXERCISE 27I: BROAD PRONOUN REFERENCE

This exercise should be done after reading Section 27.5.2 in the *Handbook*.
Revise the following sentences to correct the broad pronoun reference.

1.   In *Colorado Carpet*, the court held that an oral contract for ordinary carpet was unenforceable. The *Colorado Carpet* court reasoned that there was no evidence to indicate that the carpet was specially made for the buyer because it could be found in other retail outlets. The defendant tried to use this to say that the towels, like the carpet, are not special.

2.   The defense could bring up evidence of large sales of happy face items during the happy face fad several years ago. However, the happy face fad no longer exists, which weakens this argument.

3.   The defense counsel addressed the subject of silence during direct examination of the defendant, which opened the door for a further development of the subject.

4.   The trial court admitted the defendant's prior convictions for theft because they proved only that the defendant acted in conformity with his propensity to commit crimes, which is prohibited by ER 404(b).

5.   The destruction of the rosebushes could be classified as permanent, which would make the school district liable for the difference in the value of the Archers' property before and after the damage.

6.   The Washington State Constitution expressly forbids the in-court questioning of witnesses about their religious beliefs for the purpose of affecting the weight of their testimony. Wash. Const. art. I, § 11. This is repeated and underscored by Washington Rule of Evidence 610.

7.   In the present case, the prosecution asked the prosecuting witness several questions about her religious activities, beliefs, and opinions, bolstering her credibility with the jury at the expense of Mr. Doughtery's due process rights. (RP 151-52). U.S. Const. amend. XIV; Wash. Const. art. I § 22. In allowing this, the trial court committed an error of constitutional magnitude. *See Thomas*, 130 Ariz. at 435, 436 636 P.2d at 1217-18; *Estabrook*, 162 Or. at 101, 91 P.2d at 850.

8. Thus, the prosecution used the witness's religious beliefs, which had nothing to do with the issues before the trial court, to make her testimony seem more credible than Mr. Doughtery's testimony. Such is prohibited under Wash. Const. art I, § 11 and ER 610.

9. Under ER 609(a)(2), when a trial court admits prior conviction evidence of a crime that does not contain an element of deceit, fraud, or false swearing, the trial court commits an error of constitutional magnitude. *State v. Harris*, 102 Wash. 2d 148, 685 P.2d 584 (1984). The rationale for this is that while crimes of dishonesty bear directly on a defendant's propensity for truthfulness, other types of crimes do not bear on truthfulness and their admission might serve to prejudice the jury against the defendant.

10. The trial court did not give a cautionary accomplice instruction. This court held that such is required whenever the prosecution relies solely on accomplice testimony.

EXERCISE 27J: PRONOUN ANTECEDENTS

This exercise should be done after reading Section 27.5.3 in the *Handbook.*

Revise the following sentences so that all pronouns have noun antecedents.

1. The Bloomquists' pre-marital agreement states that they consider Mr. Bloomquist's residuals to be community property.

2. In Freeman's book, *The Grammatical Lawyer*, he discusses numerous rules of usage.

3.   From the board's minutes, we can infer that it knew about the structural weaknesses in the building and decided not to act.

4.   An attorney's notes from a client interview must be protected under the work-product rule; otherwise, the opposition will have access to the strategy he or she plans to use in the   case.

5.   According to petitioner's testimony, he did not deliberately shoot anyone.

EXERCISE 27K: PRONOUN REVIEW

This exercise should be done after reading Section 27.5 in the *Handbook*.

Correct all the problems with pronouns in the following sentences.

1.   In *Finch*, the petitioner's vehicle collided with the respondent's. He submitted a claim for property damage to respondent's insurance carrier, which he agreed to pay.

2.   Anita Hempstead is a single mother with an 18-month-old daughter. The lights and noise from the night baseball prevent her from sleeping. This occurs twice a week. Consequently, Ms. Hempstead claims that the loss of sleep interrupts her entire weekly schedule.

3.   Upon receipt of Wilson's case, the prosecutor's office treated it in the same fashion as all other referrals. That included processing the police reports, screening them for legal sufficiency, typing and filing an information, and setting an arraignment date with proper notice. Once he realized that it could not be

routinely processed in the twelve business days between receipt of the police reports and Wilson's eighteenth birthday, he referred the case to the adult division for filing charges.

4.   In May of 2009, the president of Glad Tidings Towel Company (GTT) telephoned the president of Smokey Stover Hotels (SSH) to say that he was now responsible for the order and to inform him that GTT had completed 20,000 of the 50,000 towels ordered. This surprised him because he had never signed a contract ordering the towels, which is company policy.

EXERCISE 27L: MODIFIER PLACEMENT

This exercise should be done after reading Section 27.6.1 in the *Handbook.*

Using the single word modifiers in parentheses, move the modifier to several positions in the sentence and explain the resulting change in meaning.

1.   The deputy prosecutor asked that the plaintiff describe his assailant. (JUST)

2.   The defendant claims that the plaintiff was sleeping. (ONLY)

EXERCISE 27M: MODIFIER PLACEMENT

This exercise should be done after reading Section 27.6.1 in the *Handbook.*

In the following sentences, decide where the modifiers should be placed.

1.   After Mr. Harper pays alimony and child support, he has enough money to live on. (BARELY)

2.   The court stated that the unavoidable accident defense was appropriate when neither party was at fault and when the party was surprised by sudden changes in circumstances that the party could not reasonably anticipate. (ONLY)

EXERCISE 27N: MISPLACED MODIFIERS

This exercise should be done after reading Section 27.6.1 in the *Handbook.*

Revise the following sentences to correct the misplaced modifiers.

1.   The deputy marshal testified on March 12, 2009, that a copy of the complaint was served on the defendant at his Chicago residence. (Service was on March 12, 2009, not the deputy marshal's statement.)

2.   The duty of a plaintiff in a failed vasectomy is only to mitigate damages through a reasonable means; an abortion is not required.

3.   The court reasoned that many people would be willing to support the unplanned child given the chance. (Revise so that many people, not the unplanned child, are given the chance.)

4.   Acme Clothing Co. discriminated against Mary Smith when it failed to issue her a new credit card for an existing open-ended account under her maiden name. (The account was under her married name; she wants a new credit card under her maiden name.)

5. Custom-made towels ordered by the buyer imprinted with yellow happy faces trimmed in purple satisfy the requirement of specially manufactured goods.

6. Harrison Lumber Co., the plaintiff in this action, has filed suit against our client, Lloyd Putnam, for breach of contract in federal district court.

7. Hawaii currently does not restrict foreign investment in privately owned real estate; on the contrary, discrimination is prohibited in real estate transactions based on ancestry.

8. In *Rovinski v. Rowe*, Robert Rowe brought a personal injury action against Stanley Rovinski for injuries from an automobile accident that he sustained.

9. Mrs. Davidson's car collided with Mrs. Howe's car in the middle lane, which was traveling at a lawful rate of speed.

10. Although gruesome, the court held that the photographs must be considered in light of the facts needed to be proved by the prosecution.

EXERCISE 27O: DANGLING MODIFIERS

This exercise should be done after reading Section 27.6.2 in the *Handbook.*

Revise the following sentences to correct for dangling modifiers.

1. In order to answer this question, the rule that governs service of process must be examined.

2. Applying the majority rule to our facts, the benefit of the Bells having a healthy child outweighs the burden.

3. To prove discrimination, it must be shown that the only difference between our client and the others granted credit was Ms. Smith's protected classification.

4. In using the balancing test, whether the defendant testified at the prior trial must be considered.

5. Comparing *McDonald* to our case, the facts are conclusive that Komotios's identification in the police car resulted from impermissibly suggestive police actions.

6. To determine whether Acme discriminated against our client, four factors must be examined.

7. In measuring monetary damages to real property, two distinctions are made.

8.   In determining what constitutes "appreciable time," a specific or standard amount of time has not been clearly defined by the courts.

9.   Equipment designs are presented to the prospective buyer for approval. Once approved, a bid stating the contract price is submitted.

10.   In order to collect your pruning fee from Mr. Brown, filing a lien against his orchard may be the best course of action.

EXERCISE 27P: PARALLELISM

This exercise should be done after reading Section 27.7 in the *Handbook*.

Revise the following sentences so that the coordinated elements are parallel.

1.   The defense counsel elicited that the appellant paid for a listed telephone in his own name, kept some clothes and artifacts there, and the room was ready for him to be occupied.

2.   As a result of the collision, Rice suffered a severe concussion, two broken ribs, lost a front tooth, whiplash, and numerous bruises and lacerations.

3.   Provisions allowing arbitration are generally upheld because they enhance fair dealing among the parties and for the prevention of litigation.

4. Chavaria's only reasons for breaking into the locked box in the Senator's desk were his suspicion that it contained the Senator's financial records and he expected a probable reward from the Justice Department.

5. The voluminous record in this case contains both substantial and conflicting evidence regarding the sequence of events, the actions of the parties, and what was the condition of the intersection.

6. The issues for review are whether the trial court abused its discretion by not placing a value on certain items of personal property and when it ordered John to pay $600 per month in child support for his four children.

7. One factor governing the award of child support includes the cost of caring for, maintaining, and education of the children.

8. The two critical factors in the "instrument or agent" analysis of Fourth Amendment search and seizure law are whether the government knew about and acquiesced to the search and the intent of the party performing the search.

9. Clipse described the assailant as wearing a green denim outfit, glasses, and had short wavy hair.

10. To ensure that claimants would be aware of the new act, the Legislature directed the Department of Ecology to publish a statutorily prescribed notice by four different means: 1) publication of the notice once a year for five years in major

as well as local newspapers; 2) publication of the notice every six months on radio and television stations broadcasting in every county; 3) posting the notice in a conspicuous location in every county; and 4) including a copy of the notice with notices of taxes due for 1972 mailed by each county treasurer.

EXERCISE 27Q: PARALLELISM

This exercise should be done after reading Section 27.7 in the *Handbook*.

Revise the following sentences so that the coordinated elements are parallel.

1. The trial court concluded that the agreement was not only fair economically but also procedurally fair.

2. Green fibers that were found to be microscopically indistinguishable from the fibers in Nichol's t-shirt both were found in the car and on the gloves.

3. Mr. Parker claims that the trial court's actions resulted in a property distribution that was neither fair nor was it equitable.

4. The plaintiff alleges that the City failed not only to erect proper warning signs but also failed to trim obscuring vegetation at the northeast quadrant of the intersection.

5. The jury is not to consider this evidence as either proof of negligence or as an admission of negligence on the part of the City.

6. The notation on the agent's copy could mean that either Peters made only a quote to Garfield or actually obtained the excess coverage from Munson Insurance.

7. The State can neither take action that will unnecessarily "chill" the assertion of a constitutional right nor can the State draw adverse inferences from the exercise of a constitutional right.

8. In this case, the prosecutor's comments appear to extend more to the defendant's theory of mistaken identity than his guilt or innocence.

9. The State charged Mookins with one count of assault committed either by the use of a weapon or instrument likely to produce bodily harm or by knowingly inflicting grievous bodily harm upon the victim.

10. Heller did not object to the use of the medical records evidence at either the board hearing or during the trial de novo in superior court.

Chapter 28
Punctuation

Using rule 1, add commas as needed in the following sentences. If no commas are needed, simply mark the sentence as correct.

1.   McNeill was initially represented by counsel but he moved for a court-appointed attorney shortly before trial.

2.   The trial court did not abuse its discretion in allowing a uniformed deputy to be present in the courtroom and the petitioner has not shown any prejudice stemming from the exercise of this discretion.

3.   McNair admitted at the sentencing hearing that the victim was 4 years old and that he was 21 but he disputed the court's other reasons for the exceptional sentence.

4.   The record of the 1986 guilty plea hearing reflects that Wadsworth was incarcerated at the time of his attempted escape and that he understood the elements of the escape charge and its possible punishment.

5.   Numerous people complained to Dr. Pao about the billing practices yet he expressed his approval and encouraged continuation of the practices.

6.   The defendant's associates are known to have Mafia connections and one has a reputation for deadly violence.

7.   Olmsted was aware of the charges against him and the record reflects that he knowingly waived his constitutional rights before entering a guilty plea.

8.   The cocaine's wholesale value was $17,000 and its street value was $80,000.

9.   The invasion of Jones's rights appears to be minimal for it was Jones herself who directed the officer to retrieve the identification from her purse.

10.   The president of Clearwater Mutual Savings Association demanded that the *Times* print a retraction of the false story but the *Times* refused to do so.

Exercise 28B: Commas -- Rule 2

Using rule 2, add commas as needed in the following sentences. If there are no errors, simply mark the sentence as correct.

1.   To convict the defendant of the crime charged the court must find that he had actual knowledge that he was possessing stolen property.

2.   In response to DuPont's request Hommel agreed to accompany DuPont to the rear of the store.

3.   Viewing the evidence in a light most favorable to the prosecution the trial court found the essential elements of the crime.

4.   In the early morning hours of December 3, 2009, officers from the Houston Police Department were dispatched to an abandoned railroad depot.

5.   Furthermore the trial court cautioned the jury to scrutinize separately each defendant's case.

6.   Moreover to ensure that claimants would be aware of the new act the legislature directed the Department of Ecology to publish a statutorily prescribed notice.

7.   If there is probable cause police may extend a warrantless search to containers in cars. *California v. Acevedo*, 500 U.S. 565 (1991).

8.   In *Beck* the U.S. Supreme Court held that the death sentence may not constitutionally be imposed for a capital offense when the jury was not permitted to consider any lesser included offenses.

9.   After waiving his right to a speedy trial six times Martin pleaded guilty to the crime of indecent liberties.

10.   However if the evidence is admissible for one of these purposes the trial court must determine whether the danger of undue prejudice from its admission outweighs the probative value of the evidence.

Exercise 28C: Commas -- Rule 3

Using rule 3, add commas as needed in the following sentences. If there are no errors, simply mark the sentence as correct.

1.   Of the twenty two witnesses are willing to testify.

2.   During a surveillance on three successive evenings police officers observed people exchanging cash for packaged articles.

3.   Two years before the car's brakes failed on a steep mountain road.

4.   Once he had the idea that all women were laughing at him behind his back.

5.   Without a doubt about half the witnesses to the accident will be unwilling to get involved.

Exercise 28D: Commas -- Rule 4

Using rule 4, add commas as needed in the following sentences. If there are no errors, simply mark the sentence as correct.

1.   Trooper Yessler who investigated the accident testified that the "primary causal factor" of the accident was Neimeyer's intoxicated state.

2.   The state trooper who investigated the accident testified that the "primary causal factor" of the accident had been Neimeyer's intoxicated state.

3.   The Washington State legislature enacted RCW 28A.605.020 which requires school districts to develop a policy to allow parents to access their child's school.

4.   The police talked with a neighbor who had seen a man matching Daniels's description within a block of the Wyatt home on the day of the burglary.

5.   At about 10:30 p.m., Officer Underwood encountered Norman Rhemn whom she had observed driving by several times during the evening.

6.   Did the trial court err in giving instruction 9 which sets forth the circumstances permitting the jury to find whether the petitioner had "actual knowledge" that he possessed stolen property?

7.   Those who fail to file waive their water rights.

8.   The defendant's conviction was reversed on the ground that the informant was a material witness who could not be subpoenaed by the defense. *Id.* at 1146.

9.   The State appealed to Division Two of the Court of Appeals which reversed and remanded in a published opinion filed August 5, 2004.

10.   A polygraph examination is a reasonable extension of those statutory conditions that require a probationer to follow the instructions of his or her probation officer. *See, e.g.,* Wash. Rev. Code § 9.95.210.

Exercise 28E: Commas -- Rule 4

Explain the difference in meaning in the following pairs of sentences.

1a.   Barley & Barnes argued that independent contractors who performed the actual dredging were responsible for any negligence.

1b.   Barley & Barnes argued that independent contractors, who performed the actual dredging, were responsible for any negligence.

2a.   Defense counsel will discuss all of the factors that favor exclusion of prior conviction evidence.

2b.   Defense counsel will discuss all of the factors, which favor exclusion of prior conviction evidence.

3a.   Based on that information, the detectives checked for the serial number, which was missing.

3b.   Based on that information, the detectives checked for the serial number that was missing.

Exercise 28F: Commas -- Rules 5 and 6

Using rules 5 and 6, add commas as needed in the following sentences. If there are no errors, simply mark the sentence as correct.

1.   The State has charged the defendant with dealing in a controlled substance a Class B felony.

2.   The State opposed the motion arguing that the defendant should have filed a personal restraint petition.

3.   The only witness Ann Peters had discussed her potential criminal liability with the prosecutor.

4.   Contending that his prior guilty pleas were constitutionally invalid Lemons moved to vacate the remaining habitual criminal order.

5.   Petitioner Christopher Landa seeks review of a Court of Appeals decision affirming his conviction for second degree burglary.

6.   Olson claims that a new trial should have been granted because Nyles the victim was available to testify.

7.   Supreme Court Justices Thomas and Scalia voted against granting certiorari.

8.   Campbell's most recent conviction was for second degree assault the same crime he is currently charged with committing.

9.   Holding that the facts were sufficient to require the submission of the defense of duress to the jury the Court of Appeals reversed stating that "[t]he time has come when we can no longer close our eyes to the growing problem of institutional gang rapes in our prison system."

10.   Olsen appealed to the Court of Appeals assigning error to the fact that the trial court permitted "the presence of uniformed deputies in the courtroom." *See* Appellant Br. at 6.

Exercise 28G: Commas -- Rules 7 and 8

Using rules 7 and 8, add commas as needed in the following sentences. If there are no errors, simply mark the sentence as correct.

1.   When asked whether he and O'Malley were aware that Tanner had a gun, Swanson replied "Sure."

2.   One could infer therefore that the billing procedures were there for her to see.

3.   If your answers to both of these questions is "yes" then the defendant was negligent.

4.   The evidence is admissible under ER 402, which states that "[a]ll relevant evidence is admissible . . . ."

5.   Roberts however asserts that she was amenable to process at all times.

6.   Other cases on the other hand suggest that the evidence necessary to satisfy the second prong of the *Workman* test may come from any source.

7.   The trial court concluded that "Zeblowski was not so intoxicated that he did not comprehend or intend his acts."

8.   The trial court concluded "Zeblowski was not so intoxicated that he did not comprehend or intend his acts."

9.   An appellate court may on its own initiative or by motion of a party request additional evidence before rendering a decision on a case.

10.   In *Alford*, the United States Supreme Court held that a plea of guilty is constitutionally valid in spite of a defendant's claim of innocence when there was strong evidence of guilt before the trial court and when the plea was a voluntary and an intelligent choice among the alternative courses of action open to a defendant. 400 U.S. at 37-38.

Exercise 28H: Commas--Rules 9 and 10

Using rules 9 and 10, add commas as needed in the following sentences. If there are no errors, simply mark the sentence as correct.

1.   Yesler later identified James in a photo montage in a lineup and at trial.

2.   The evidence shows that the defendant was only present at the crime scene not "ready to assist."

3.   The prosecutor's comment of disbelief was directed at the defense theory of mistaken identity not at the credibility of a witness.

4.   Thompson pulled his gun held it straight up in the air and told Lew not to bring anyone back.

5.   Thus, the 90-day "time for trial" rule under CR 3.3(c)(1) began to run when Lewis was arraigned not when the State filed the information.

6.   The sanity commission concluded that Thomas was incapable of perceiving the nature of his conduct at the time of the offense was unable to distinguish right from wrong but was competent to stand trial.

7.   The court must follow United States Supreme Court decisions not a decision by the New Mexico Court of Appeals when determining whether a defendant is a public or private figure.

8.   The *Harris* court held that such an instruction is required whenever the prosecution relies solely on accomplice testimony but that failure to give the instruction is not reversible error when there is sufficient corroborating testimony.

9. Chavez saw a man on the ground but was unable to identify him because of the darkness.

10. Jeffreys was arrested for armed robbery yet was also charged later with second degree burglary.

Exercise 28I: Commas -- Rules 11 and 12

Using rules 11 and 12, add commas as needed in the following sentences. Revise sentences if necessary. If there are no errors, simply mark the sentence as correct.

1. She was taken into custody on May 11 2009 and arraigned on May 12 2009.

2. The documents in question mysteriously disappeared from the Dallas office on December 2 2008 only to reappear in the Clovis New Mexico office on December 9.

3. Bennett purchased 12 acres of remote undeveloped land in central Florida in 1997.

4. Secret unexpressed intentions are irrelevant.

5. Each applicant was required to enclose a self-addressed stamped envelope with the application form.

6. Johnston moved to Las Vegas Nevada in February 2006 to attend school.

7. The publisher mailed the contract on 1 March 2008 to the author at her Cincinnati Ohio address.

8. "Substantial evidence" exists if it is "sufficient . . . to persuade a fair-minded, rational person of the truth of a declared premise." *See Davis v. Microsoft Corp.,* 149 Wn.2d 521, 531, 70 P.2d 126 (2003).

9. Peterson filed his motion to vacate on October 26 2008 more than two years after the trial court entered the judgment of acquittal.

10. People who received one of these letters were told to "mail $5.00 to the last name and address on the list," which was Amy Andersen 1813 South Washington Lawrence Kansas 66044, or they would suffer "bad luck and other misfortune."

Exercise 28J: Commas -- Rules 11 and 12

Using rules 13, 14 and 15, add commas as needed in the following sentences. Revise sentences if necessary. If there are no errors, simply mark the sentence as correct.

1.   The white envelope contained 100 hits of acid; the blue another 100 hits.

2.   A jury entered two habitual criminal findings each based on the same prior convictions.

3.   The prosecutor has two choices in cases such as Jerome's namely proceed under Wash. Rev. Code 9.94A.825 and 9.94A.510 by charging possession of a firearm and, upon a finding to that effect, increase the presumptive range by 12 months or not charge possession of a firearm and seek an exceptional sentence under Wash. Rev. Code 9.94A.535.

4.   The adverse claimant must assert possession in a "hostile" manner; that is he or she must assert the claim against all others, including the owner of record.

5.   A person who dies intestate—that is without a valid will—leaves his or her family a legacy of woe.

6.   Melvin Andersen is listed as the president of the corporation; Philip Andersen the vice-president; Teresa Andersen the vice-president of internal affairs, and Mary Andersen the treasurer.

7.   Her only source of income cut off Irene Culver had no choice but to return to the street.

8.   McGurk's will did not specify heirs for numerous valuable possessions e.g. a three-carat diamond, 1500 shares of Microsoft, a 110 foot yacht, and a Rolls Royce.

9.   Her surgery having been labeled "successful" Glenda Jefferson checked out of the hospital and returned home.

10. The person made four identical calls the first less than two hours after the incident.

Exercise 28K: Unnecessary Commas

Using rule 16, add or delete commas as needed in the following sentences. Revise sentences if necessary. If there are no errors, simply mark the sentence as correct.

1.   A statute of frauds defense can be raised, if the employment contract is determined to have a definite term and if the contract cannot be performed within a year.

2.   Plaintiff's motion for summary judgment should be denied, when a genuine issue of material fact exists.

3.   The court will hold that the contract is void because the parole evidence will satisfy the statute of frauds requirement.

4.   The light fixture shattered and fell, as Pearson entered the room.

5.   An employer can be liable in tort for wrongful discharge if the employee's discharge "contravenes a clear mandate of public policy."

6.   There is circumstantial evidence to support the fact that Dr. Deaver encouraged fraudulent billing practices although there is no direct evidence connecting him to those practices.

7.   Ramparts, Inc. will immediately release the documents requested, unless the court enjoins such an action.

8.   A defendant does not act improperly when the defendant has a financial interest in the business of the person induced

9.   The plaintiff is unlikely to succeed in her defamation claim, because the defendant's statement was true and because the statement does not have defamatory meaning.

10.   In both *LeFever* and *Dowling*, this court held that the retrial of a defendant is barred when a trial court dismisses a case for insufficient evidence even though that ruling may be erroneous.

Exercise 28L: Unnecessary Commas

Using rules 17, 18, 19, and 20, add or delete commas as needed in the following sentences. Revise sentences if necessary. If there are no errors, simply mark the sentence as correct.

1. The police put a "trap" on the phone, so, when the man called the next day, the police were able to trace the call.

2. The Hoffelmeirs will probably receive not only the replacement value of the cat, but also compensation for their mental anguish.

3. Defendants may argue that, precisely because the plaintiff operates its business in the small community of Lincoln, it holds a position of special prominence in that community sufficient to make it an all-purpose public figure.

4. The intensity of the fire, the danger of injury from the propane tanks, and the condition and construction of the barn, mean that the fire could reasonably be classified as "manifestly dangerous."

5. The *Barr* decision is entitled to much weight in Washington both because it was decided by the full bench of the Washington Supreme Court, and because there was no dissenting opinion.

6. Either she stole the car from the parking lot, or she mistook it for a friend's car.

7. Wells's claim that he was denied his right to cross-examine the representatives of the third-party payors who testified about the payment restrictions, could be valid if he was prevented from negating any inference that he knew the billings were fraudulent.

8. The court held that, when there is a period of delay between filing the information and the arraignment, the time for trial set forth in Cr 2.2 (c)(1) begins to run the date the information is filed.

9. The court ruled that, although the form was incorrect, the substantive information supplied by the claimant met the legislative intent by "providing adequate records for administration of the state's waters and notifying the State that the water was being put to beneficial use." *Id.* at 704.

10. Neither did the trial court abuse its discretion, nor did it err in admitting photographs of the defendant with dental retractors in his mouth.

Using all the comma rules in section 28.1, add or delete commas as needed in the following sentences. Revise sentences if necessary. If there are no errors, simply mark the sentence as correct.

1.   The Supreme Court held that summary judgment was proper, because the State's actions in failing to perform the eye examination, and noting an appropriate restriction were totally unrelated to the accident.

2.   At the disposition hearing, the State presented a document describing Nowell's prior criminal history which consisted of twelve burglary convictions and two minor offenses subject to diversion.

3.   After checking into the Ramada Inn on Highway 12, Gates called Dates Unlimited, an escort service, and arranged for Teresa Mitton to meet him at his hotel room.

4.   Both contentions will fail, if this accident resulted without any warning of Ms. O'Toole's impending blackout.

5.   For example, if Acme conditioned employment on Mr. McIntyre participating in an illegal scheme to fix prices, plaintiff may ultimately succeed in a wrongful discharge claim.

6.   Even though the evidence does not demonstrate that Marvin and Leroy verbalized any plan to carry out the assault they both appear to have been active participants in the crime.

7.   The first instance of alleged prosecutorial misconduct occurred during closing argument, when the prosecutor made several statements concerning O'Toole's failure to call Doris Simms as an alibi witness.

8.   Owens asserts that the manufacture of a controlled substance may be accomplished only by extraction of chemical synthesis not by cultivation.

9.   On the evening of February 28 2010 Atlanta Police Officer Louise Simpson, was working undercover on prostitution detail.

10.   A waiver to the right to a jury trial must be voluntary, knowing and intelligent.

11.   Kevin Morton rode as the "spotter", the person designated to alert the boat driver when the skier falls.

12.   Defense counsel chose to present only one alibi witness, Bertha Owens, who stated that she was in Des Moines, Iowa at the time of the robbery.

13. Marie Tao, the defendant's girlfriend, was contacted by an officer who asked if the defendant was there but she denied knowing anything about his location.

14. Mason maintains that, like the convictions in *Mace*, one of his convictions was reversed on appeal, and that the habitual criminal finding must likewise be vacated.

15. The Barkers argue that, even if the statutory notice is constitutionally adequate they substantially complied with the requirements of the Water Rights Registration Act.

16. Sanchez argues in his petition for review both that the State did not have probable cause to arrest him for armed robbery without a warrant and that it could not later charge him with second degree burglary.

17. When Officer Smith asked who had been driving the cars, Pinette approached him and said "I'm the drive of the Volvo."

18. This court has warned prosecutors that it will not tolerate the admission of repetitious inflammatory photographs.

19. The Washington State Supreme Court has held that, when a case has been appealed and a judgment issued by the appellate court the trial court may not interfere "by any proceeding in the cause which is not directed by the appellate order." *State v. Graeber*, 49 Wash. 2d 874, 875, 307 P.2d 563, 563 (1957).

20. The appellant placed her daughter in a private out-of-district school in Denver Colorado without first notifying the school district.

Exercise 28N: Semicolons

Using Rule 1, substitute semicolons for commas or periods separating main clauses when it would be correct and effective to do so. If there are no errors, simply mark the sentence as correct.

1. Thorndike's permission to use his land was an oral license, therefore, he has the right to revoke the license to use his property.

2. Permission is a revocable act, it does not ripen into a prescriptive right unless the user's acts evidence a positive assertion of a right to use.

3. Duckworth neither asked for nor received permission. Therefore, his use was adverse to the true owners of the property.

4. Texas law would probably affirm Thorndike's oral license, however, there are incidents in which oral licenses have become prescriptive easements.

5. Duckworth will contend that he offered Thorndike the cord of firewood as consideration in return for the right to use the road. Thorndike will contend that his acceptance of the firewood was not intended as acceptance of consideration.

6. Neither court held for the defendant, neither court was reversed.

7. The police found a tire bar and a paper bag hidden under the house. Both had traces of blood and human hair.

8. The plaintiff's behavior was observable, he was seen actively using the boat.

9. Loren and Joseph assert that the jury linked their actions because they are cousins, therefore, their mutually antagonistic defenses made severance appropriate.

10. In *Ruona*, the defendant's car was partially in a traffic lane. In *Taylor*, the defendant's car was in a borrow pit, which is a trench alongside the road.

Exercise 28O: Semicolons

Decide which of the following sentences need a semicolon rather than a comma between the main clauses. If there are no errors, simply mark the sentence as correct.

1. The first two elements are satisfied, the third element, hostility, is not satisfied.

2. The first two elements are satisfied, but the third element, hostility, is not satisfied.

3. The first two elements are satisfied, however, the third element, hostility, is not satisfied.

4. Although the first two elements are satisfied, the third element, hostility, is not satisfied.

5. The first two elements are satisfied; the third element, however, is not satisfied.

6.	Thus, if Jones was acting as a private individual, the evidence he obtained will be admitted; if, however, the court finds requisite government involvement in the search, the evidence may be suppressed.

7.	The Justice Department will argue that Jones was acting as a private individual; therefore, the evidence he obtained should be admitted. If the court finds requisite government involvement in the search; however, the evidence will be suppressed.

8.	If Jones was acting as a private individual, then the evidence he obtained will be admitted, however, if the court finds requisite involvement in the search, then the evidence may be suppressed.

9.	Although the evidence Jones obtained may be admitted if he was acting as a private individual, the court will probably find that he acted as a government agent and that there was requisite government involvement in the search; therefore, the evidence probably will be suppressed.

10.	The evidence Jones obtained will be admitted only if he was acting as a private individual; the evidence will be suppressed only if the court finds requisite involvement in the search.

Exercise 28P: Semicolons

Replace commas with semicolons in the following sentences if the items in the series are long or if one or more of the items has internal commas. If there are no errors, simply mark the sentence as correct.

1.	The reasonableness test includes several factors: the location of the business, the degree of interference with another business, and the test of sensibilities, that is, whether a person of ordinary sensibilities would be offended.

2.	Remedies for private nuisance include abatement by warrant, injunctions, damages, which are measured by the loss suffered by the plaintiff, or declaratory judgment.

3.   The court used several factors in its balancing test: the character of the neighborhood, the ratio of complaining to noncomplaining tenants, and the possible interference with the tenants' comfortable enjoyment of life, with their right to privacy, and with their use of the property as an apartment.

4.   The defendant will point to the following facts to prove he is operating his business lawfully: (1) he has satisfied all necessary zoning and licensing requirements, including the special requirements imposed by the waterfront commission, (2) the fitness club's activities do not physically invade the Harborview restaurant, and (3) the activities do not harm anybody.

5.   Three elements of the statute must be examined:

       1.   the driver must be intoxicated;
       2.   the driver must be in actual physical control of a motor vehicle, and
       3.   the motor vehicle must be on a public highway.

Exercise 28Q: Semicolon Review

Read the following sentences and decide whether the underlined punctuation is correct as is or whether it should be changed. If correct, simply mark the sentence "correct." If changes in punctuation are required, indicated what punctuation marks should be used.

1.   A true emergency did exist, consequently, there was no time for deliberation.

2.   The viability of a fetus is based on several factors: the health of the mother and child, the weight and race of the fetus, available life-sustaining techniques, and the length of the pregnancy, when the length can be determined.

3.   In *Green*, the court refused to rule as a matter of law that a fourteen-week-old fetus was non-viable; because the court held that viability was a factual issue that must be decided by a jury.

4.   In a similar case, a defendant's failure to signal his intention to make a left hand turn violated the turn signal statute; but the defendant was not liable for the accident because the speed of the other car, not the defendant's failure to signal, was found to be the proximate cause of the accident.

5. Whether to award damages is entirely up to the court's discretion, the court has the option of awarding attorneys' fees to the party who wins the case, but it is not obligated to do so.

6. The jury will find that Mr. Cutter's assessment of the situation was reasonable, therefore, he was not negligent.

7. If these elements are not met, the plaintiff could not maintain an action under public nuisance, but he could still consider a cause of action under private nuisance, which is broadly defined as "every nuisance not included in the definition" of public nuisance.

8. Private nuisance affects the rights of a limited community. Public nuisance affects the rights of the entire community.

9. The Washington Supreme Court has addressed the issue of injury and wrongful death of a fetus and allowed recovery for both; recovery, however, has always been for a "viable fetus."

10. To seize evidence under the plain view doctrine, police officers must satisfy the following requirements:

    (1) they must have "prior justification for intrusion";
    (2) they must come across the evidence "inadvertently";
    (3) they must immediately recognize "that they have evidence before them."

Exercise 28R: Colons

In the following sentences, add or delete colons as needed. If there are no errors, simply mark the sentence as correct. In some cases, additional words will needed to be added to create a grammatically complete lead-in.

1. A two-part inquiry is used to determine reliability (1) was the confrontation procedure suggestive, and (2) under the totality of circumstances, was the identification reliable even if the confrontation procedure was suggestive?

2. Officials who are accorded absolute immunity seem to share one common characteristic they make discretionary decisions in an adversarial proceeding under time and information constraints.

3. In California, the service-oriented businesspersons subject to the bulk sales law are the baker, the cafe or restaurant owner, the garage owner, and the cleaner and dyer.

4. By requiring independent corroborating evidence only in *Miranda* situations, the court has adopted what seems to be a radical approach admissions made in a pre-*Miranda* setting, at least in DWI cases, do not need corroborating evidence.

5. The defendant is accused of assaulting Agnes Miller, Denise Donovan, Ellie Emory, and Christine Fremont.

6. The court found that the prosecutor's comments during her closing argument were not improper because (1) the witness was "peculiarly available" to the defendant and would have been able to elucidate the events of the crime; (2) the witness has pleaded guilty to a prior crime on the condition that he would not be prosecuted for the crimes charged; and (3) the defendant repeatedly attempted to place responsibility for the charged incident on the witness. *Id*. at 628.

7. An investigation revealed that five individuals were at the railroad depot on the night Jones was assaulted; Francis O'Connor, Noel O'Connor, Phillip Whalen, Paul Mendoza, and Tony Rialto.

8. The trial court gave the following reasons justifying the exceptional sentence:

    1. The defendant has been in and out of the criminal justice system since the mid-1960s;

    2. Even while under probation, the defendant has committed crime after crime, which is an affront to the court's purpose of protecting the public and ensuring the protection of law;

    3. The defendant is a danger to society through his theft and burglary of the property of others and possession of firearms while under felony convictions;

    4. Probation is not a viable alternative; while under probation, the defendant has continued to commit felonies. CP 14.

9.   The court in *Petersen* reasoned that a separate covenant is implied between the seller and purchaser: "because of the unusual dependent relationship of the vendee to the vendor." *Id.* at 1158.

11. For the court to have found for the plaintiffs in *Kelley*, the plaintiffs would have had to establish:

1.   the condominium conversion required "extensive rehabilitative construction";

2.   the defects complained of by the condominium owners were defects of the "new" construction; and

3.   the defects complained of were "latent" defects.

Exercise 28S: Apostrophes

Using apostrophes, form the possessive of the following underlined nouns.

1. judge error

2. judges errors

3. prosecuting attorney assistant

4. son-in-law employer

5. it

6. Terry and Howard children (joint possession)

7. Terry and Howard children (individual possession)

8. Lois complaint

9. fringe benefits value

10. two weeks vacation

Exercise 28T: Apostrophes

Using apostrophes, form the plural possessive of each of the following words.

1. agency

2. Mathews

3. security

4. Davis

5. bar examiner

Exercise 28U: Apostrophes

Use apostrophes to form the possessive, the plural, or the plural possessive, as indicated, of the following underlined words.

1.   100 (form plural)

2.   prostitute clientele (form plural possessive)

3.   electrician union (form plural possessive)

4.   franchise securities (form singular possessive)

5.   Doris and Thomas executors (individual possession)

6.   for old times sake (form possessive)

7.   change the Mary to Mari (form the plural of both)

8.   promissory note validity (form singular possessive)

9.   policy effects (form plural possessive)

10.   tenant organization (form plural possessive)

11.   Schultz automobile (form singular possessive)

12.   Schultz automobile (form plural possessive)

13.   boss meeting (form plural possessive)

14.   the <u>Mayor of New York</u> statement (form possessive)

15.   <u>Clinton & Nelson</u> construction company (form joint possessive)

16.   <u>1990</u> (form plural)

17.   <u>justice of the peace</u> decision (form possessive)

18.   too many <u>if</u> (form plural)

19.   <u>somebody else</u> problem (form possessive)

20.   <u>who</u> (form possessive)

Exercise 28V: Other Marks of Punctuation

Find and correct the errors in quotation marks, ellipses, brackets, and parentheses in the following sentences. If there are no errors, simply mark the sentence as correct.

1.   The word "aid" means all assistance whether given by words, acts, encouragement, support, or presence.

2.   The hearing examiner found the zoning code to be slightly ambiguous:

> It is clear that this controversy could have been avoided if the zoning code definition presented more specific information as to whether the fee underlying a street should be included in lot area calculations.

CP 60-61.

3.   Summary judgment ". . . shall be rendered forthwith if the pleadings, depositions, answers to interrogatories, and admissions on file, together with the affidavits, if any, show that there is no genuine issue as to any material fact and that the moving party is entitled to a judgment as a matter of law." Fed. R. Civ. P. 56(c).

4.   As noted in *Coolidge*, the scope of a search is limited, and officers must have justification for being in a position to view the incriminating evidence:

> "[I]t is important to keep in mind that, in the vast majority of cases, any evidence seized by the police will be in plain view, at least at the moment of seizure. The problem with the 'plain view' doctrine has been to identify the circumstances in which plain view has legal significance rather than being simply the normal concomitant of any search, legal or illegal."

403 U.S. at 465.

5.   Using the standard enunciated in *Berenson*, the *Kurzius* court held that "A zoning ordinance will be invalidated on both constitutional and state statutory grounds if it was enacted with an exclusionary purpose, or it ignores regional needs and has an unjustifiably exclusionary effect." *Id.* at 343, 414 N.E.2d at 682.

Exercise 28W: Hyphens

Add hyphens to the following phrases as needed. If there is no error, simply mark the phrase as correct.

1.   posthumous work

2.   non stock corporation

3.   multinational corporation

4.   six month lease

5.   poorly reasoned opinion

6.   ex husband

7.   extremely volatile solution

8.   all inclusive report

9.   ex parte proceeding

10.   fact finding commission

11.   priest penitent privilege

12. low to moderate-income housing

13. Hanson's case falls within an area of law that is well settled.

14. Hanson's case falls within a well-settled area of law.

15. The State has Howard's taped statement, which could be used during cross examination.

Exercise 28X: Comma Splices and Fused Sentences

Determine whether each of the following sentences contains a comma spice or is a fused sentence. If the sentence has either problem, correct it by rewriting the sentence. If the sentence has no error, simply mark it as correct.

1. Our clients, the Kearneys, were served with a complaint by their neighbor, Mr. Bob Cratchett, who asks the court to eject the Kearneys from a ten-foot strip of land between the property of the two neighbors.

2. Mr. Cratchett bought the property sometime in 2009, the facts are in dispute as to the specific month.

3. Before Mr. Cratchett bought the property, it was owned by Mrs. Moriarty she died in October 2008.

4. Since 2002, the Kearneys have used the property in a variety of ways, for example, they have regularly mowed the grass in the disputed area since 2002 or 2003.

5. The Kearneys have maintained the picnic area over the years and have used it almost daily during the summer months.

6. During the time period from 20022 to 2003, they ejected any trespassers when those trespassers tried to use the picnic area.

7. When the Kearneys built the patio area, they did not ask Mrs. Moriarty for permission, Mrs. Moriarty did not object to their use of the area before or after the patio was built.

8.	Mrs. Moriarty, however, used the picnic area for her own family picnics, although not as frequently as the Kearneys.

9.	The Kearneys did not get along with Mr. Cratchett in the way they did with Mrs. Moriarty because he had loud parties and because he let his dogs run free.

10.	Mr. Cratchett believed that the boundary line between the two properties was the retaining wall that had been mistakenly extended onto Mr. Moriarty's property, however, in October 2009, he had his land surveyed and learned the true property line.

Chapter 29
Mechanics

There are no exercises for this chapter.

Chapter 30
Before You Practice

There are no exercises for this chapter.

Chapter 31
English as a Second Language Grammar

Using the lists in Chapter 31 of *The Legal Writing Handbook,* 5th edition or Chapter 10 of *Just Writing,* 3rd edition or an ESL dictionary such as the *Longman Dictionary of Contemporary English,* determine if the underlined nouns are count or non-count nouns. Correct the sentences as needed.

1. Because <u>housing</u> costs had risen dramatically in recent years, Ms. Ankita Singh decided to rent an apartment rather than buy a <u>home</u>.

2. She selected an apartment on Clyde Hill because it was near her place of <u>employment</u> and because the location offered her considerable <u>privacies</u>.

3. The apartment was advertised as "furnished," but before Ms. Singh moved in, all the <u>furnitures,</u> including appliances like the <u>refrigerator,</u> were removed.

4. The advertisement had also stated that all utilities, including <u>electricity</u> and <u>water</u>, were included in the rent.

5. The landlord assured her that the <u>traffic</u> in the area was light and that <u>transportations</u> to and from the area were safe and reliable.

Exercise 31B: Articles -- "A" and "An"

In the following sentences, determine which is correct—"a," "an," or no article.

Officers Tony Marino and Enrique Garcia were on (a/an/no article) patrol in (a/an/no article) new housing development when they noticed (a/an/no article) two boys loitering near (a/an/no article) group of rural mailboxes. One of the boys had his back turned toward the officers, and he appeared to be opening (a/an/no article) envelope. The other boy appeared to be putting (a/an/no article) several pieces of mail in (a/an/no article) backpack. When Officer Marino stopped the patrol car and started to get out, (a/an/no article) third boy who was further down the street shouted, "Run!" The two boys near the mailboxes dropped the mail and started running into (a/an/no article) orchard on the outskirts of the housing area. Officer Marino ran after them. While in (a/an/no article) pursuit, Marino saw the second boy throw the backpack behind (a/an/no article) apple tree.

Exercise 31C: Articles – A" and "An"

"A" and "An" have been used incorrectly with non-count nouns in the following sentences. Add in a quantifier to correct the sentence. The sentences can also be corrected by omitting the article or changing the noun to a verb.

Example:

The defendant stopped at Laredo, Texas, to buy a gasoline.

Corrected:

The defendant stopped at Laredo, Texas, to buy a **few gallons of** gasoline.

or:

The defendant stopped at Laredo, Texas, to buy gasoline. (no article before "gasoline")

1.   Cosmic Toys, Inc. will be found liable for a negligence if the plaintiff can prove that it knew that its Little Tommy gun was hazardous to children.

2.   If the court does not admit an evidence of the Cosmic report on injuries sustained by children playing with the Little Tommy gun, the plaintiff's case will be seriously compromised.

31-2

3.   The plaintiff must prove that Cosmic had a knowledge that when the gun replicated the backfire of an actual weapon, some children sustained eye injuries.

4.   In addition to the Little Tommy gun, Cosmic makes guns that are toy versions of ones used when a hunting.

5.   One Cosmic toy rifle, known as NRA Junior, is made of a wood and a plastic.

6.   Cosmic has recalled the NRA Junior because, with extensive outdoor use, the wooden stock of the toy rifle suffered a deterioration, including warping and splintering.

7.   The defendant expects a testimony at trial that Cosmic has a record of recalling toys it knows to be defective.

8.   The defendant will argue that Cosmic recalls toys only when it is under an intense pressure to do so by consumers and the media.

9.   A research about Cosmic and other toy gun manufacturers gives the industry a mixed report card.

10.   The study noted that Cosmic was accused of a discrimination against its female employees.

Exercise 31D: Articles -- "The"

In the following sentences, determine if the article "the" has been used correctly. Add in "the" if it was incorrectly omitted; omit "the" if it was incorrectly added.

1. On Tuesday, April 11, 2008, Jonny Phan was driving home from his new job at Sears store in Queen City Mall.

2. Unfortunately, the quickest route home was through an area known as "red light district."

3. When Phan stopped at an intersection, two women who had been standing near the intersection waved to him.

4. The taller woman leaned into the open window on passenger side of car and asked him "if he wanted to have some fun."

5. Phan, who has difficulty understanding the American accents, was not sure that he understood her correctly.

6. Assuming the women might be in trouble or need help, Phan pulled over to the curb.

7. The taller woman told him that an hour with them would cost $100.

8. Convinced now that the women needed help, Phan reached into his wallet and handed the women a $5.00 bill.

9. Officer Peter Meyers, who was on bicycle patrol in the area, saw the money exchange hands.

10. Stopping his bike on the driver's side of the car, Officer Meyers immediately arrested Phan for soliciting prostitution.

31-4

In the following paragraphs, the articles have been omitted. Add in the correct articles as needed. Assume that the articles in the quoted material are correct.

In June 2009, Dr. Arminda Sanchez was interviewed by Dr. Jorge Padilla for position at Five Rivers Community College teaching in history department. When Dr. Sanchez asked Dr. Padilla why she was being interviewed, he replied that interview was granted because department "had to interview women." Dr. Sanchez said that response hit her "like punch in the stomach." At time, history department had only male faculty. After interview, Dr. Padilla offered Dr. Sanchez a probationary teaching position, which she accepted. She became first female hired by department in sixteen years.

In summer of 2009, Dr. Sanchez arrived at history department and noticed that she was surrounded by artwork in department hallways depicting semi-nude women. Because she was only female faculty member in department, she immediately felt uncomfortable. She was also afraid pictures would make her female students feel uncomfortable, so she took them down and filed complaint with Dr. Walter Bade, department chair. According to Dr. Bade, pictures were put up in hallway by Dr. Padilla only one week before Dr. Sanchez's arrival. Dr. Bade reported incident to Dean Norma Gernon. He also forwarded complaint to Dean Gernon.

Dean Gernon determined that artwork was "not sexually harassing"; nevertheless, she issued new policy expressly forbidding posting sexually explicit material. In response to Sanchez's complaint, Gernon told Sanchez that Sanchez was being "baited" by Dr. Padilla. She recommended that Sanchez withdraw complaint and "try to get along" with her colleagues.

Despite new policy, one week later, Dr. Padilla put up several more posters of nude women in history department hallway. Several female students and female faculty member from music department complained about posters. Feeling that she was being sexually harassed, Dr. Sanchez asked if her classes and office could be moved to another building. Dr. Bade agreed that classes could be moved, but he stated that faculty member must have office in his or her own department so Dr. Sanchez's office could not be moved.

By middle of fall semester, Dr. Sanchez and Dr. Padilla had met several times to resolve their differences. In first meeting, Dr. Padilla insisted that pornography "was liberating to women" and argued that only unenlightened individual would complain about artwork. In second meeting, he listened to Dr. Sanchez for few minutes and then abruptly stood up, said "the department was better to a man before you came," and then left room. In their final meeting, Dr. Padilla told her that good colleague would not complain about small things such as few posters and that she needed man in her life "to loosen her up."

Two days after final meeting with Dr. Padilla, Dr. Sanchez filed formal complaint of sexual harassment with Dean Gernon and Equal Employment Opportunity Commission (EEOC).

Exercise 31F: Auxiliary, or Helping Verbs

Using the auxiliary, or helping, verb lists in Chapter 30 of *The Legal Writing Handbook,* 5th edition, Chapter 10 of *Just Writing*, 3rd edition, or an ESL dictionary such as the *Longman Dictionary of Contemporary English,*, select the auxiliary, or helping, verb that conveys the meaning indicated in the parenthetical following the sentence.

1. States (can/should) be sued for damages for not making courthouses accessible to persons with disabilities. *(desired meaning: the action is a possibility or an option)*

2. In its 2005 ruling on Washington State's sentencing guidelines, the United States Supreme Court decided the juries, not judges, (must/will) consider each fact that could lengthen a prisoner's sentence. *(desired meaning: the action is required)*

3.   The sentencing guidelines decision (could/ought to) affect thousands of prison sentences.   *(desired meaning: the action is a possibility)*

4.   Although federal judges have a lifetime appointment, they (can/would) be impeached for misconduct.   *(desired meaning: the action is a possibility or an option)*

5.   In the past, Senators (might/would) filibuster when they lacked the votes to prevent confirmation but they believed that a president's judicial nominee was unsuitable. *(desired meaning: the action was repeated in the past)*

Exercise 31G: Base Form of Verbs

Select the correct form of the main verb in the following sentences.

1.   When the Supreme Court disqualified a constitutional challenge to the phrase "one nation under God" in the Pledge of Allegiance, it did not (rule/ruled) on the issue of whether the phrase violated the constitutional ban on establishing an official government religion.

2.   The lawsuit was (bring/brought) by a father who was an atheist and who objected to his daughter having to say the Pledge of Allegiance in school.

3.   Because the father did not have custody of the daughter, the court could (disqualify/disqualified) the challenge because the father did not have standing to bring the suit.

4.   United States district court and court of appeals judges follow a code of ethics with guidelines about when they should (disqualify/disqualified) themselves from hearing a case.

5.   In contrast, Supreme Court justices determine for themselves when, based on a conflict of interest, they will (recuse/recused) themselves from a case.

6.   In 2005, Sierra Club attorneys questioned whether Justice Antonin Scalia could (remain/remained) impartial on a case involving Vice President Cheney after Scalia and Cheney went on a hunting trip together.

7.   Justice Scalia issued a 21-page memo explaining he had not (discuss/discussed) the case with Vice President Cheney.

8.   The case involved access to meeting records from the Bush administration's energy task force that was (head/headed) by Vice President Cheney.

9.   In a 7-2 vote, the Court decided that Vice President Cheney was not (require/ required) to turn over records from the energy task force meetings.

10.   Following the decision, Chief Justice William Rehnquist appointed a committee that will (study/studied) procedures for handling ethics complaints against federal judges.

Exercise 31H: Verbs with Gerunds and Infinitives

Determine whether the verbs in the following sentences should be followed by the gerund or infinitive form.

1.   In 2004, the Supreme Court ruled that the 1998 Child Online Protection Act appeared (to violate/violating) the constitutional right to free speech.

2.   The authors of the Act intended (to prevent/preventing) children from viewing sexually explicit material on the Internet.

3.   Website operators could avoid (to pay/paying) fines of up to $50,000 by requiring users to prove they were adults.

4.   The Act permitted adults (to access/accessing) the sexually material if they used a credit card.

5.   Because the ruling was a 5-4 vote, the federal government may attempt (to bring/bringing) the case to trial again in lower court.

Answers to Practice Book Exercises

Chapter 22
Paragraphs

Although the original author of this paragraph did in fact write it as one paragraph, most readers would agree that even with the frequent signposts ("the first exception," "in the present case," "the second exception," and "in the present case") this paragraph is too long for readers to assimilate comfortably.

There are a number of ways to break this selection into shorter paragraphs, including the two that follow.

Option 1

There are some limited exceptions to the prohibitive rule stated in the above cases; however, the facts of the present case do not fall into those exceptions.

The first exception allows the questioning of a witness about religious beliefs when those beliefs are relevant to some issue other than the credibility of the witness. *State v. Stone*, 728 P.2d 674 (Ariz. Ct. App. 1986). In the present case, Ms. Patten's religious activities and beliefs were not at issue and the only conceivable purpose that the prosecution could have had for questioning her about them was to bolster her credibility by impressing the jury with her religiousness.

The second exception applies when reference to the religious beliefs of a witness is isolated and not significant to the trial proceedings in their entirety. *Id*. at 678. In the present case, the prosecution's questions--over repeated objections--about Ms. Patten's religious beliefs, as well as the closing argument comments about those beliefs, cannot be deemed isolated and inadvertent. (RP 151-52, 186).

Under the third exception, inquiry about the religious beliefs of a witness will not give rise to constitutional error if the assigning party invites the error. *People v. Baseer*, 90 Ill. App. 3d 866, 414 N.E.2d 5 (1980). Hence, when a defendant testifies as to his own religious beliefs in an attempt to bolster his credibility, he will not be heard to complain when the prosecution cross-examines him about his beliefs. *Id.* at 871, 414 N.E.2d at 10. In the present case, Mr. Davidson's counsel never attempted to question Ms. Patten about her religious beliefs so as to affect her credibility, so it cannot be said that the defense "opened the door" to the prosecution's questioning of Ms. Patten about her religious beliefs. *Id.*

In short, none of the exceptions apply. Therefore, the trial court's allowance of the prosecution's questioning was an error of constitutional magnitude.

Option 2 (same as option 1 except paragraphs 1 and 2 are combined)

There are some limited exceptions to the prohibitive rule stated in the above cases; however, the facts of the present case do not fall into those exceptions. The first exception allows the questioning of a witness about religious beliefs when those beliefs are relevant to some issue other than the credibility of the witness. *State v. Stone*, 728 P.2d 674 (Ariz. Ct. App. 1986). In the present case, Ms. Patten's religious activities and beliefs were not at issue and the only conceivable purpose that the prosecution could have had for questioning her about them was to bolster her credibility by impressing the jury with her religious.

EXERCISE 22B: PARAGRAPH LENGTH

Paragraph 1 would work better if divided into two paragraphs. Divide between the second and third sentences. The first two sentences provide background information. The next three sentences focus on the complaint and possible remedies.

Although the paragraph about Mr. Baker is a one-sentence paragraph, it works well because the writer has chosen to use a separate paragraph to describe each plaintiff's complaints.

The one-sentence paragraph at the end of the statement of facts, however, is ineffective. Obviously, the writer had one additional significant fact but did not know where to put it. Because it is a background fact, it is probably best to work it into the opening paragraph, which includes other background facts.

Possible Revision of opening paragraph:

> Despite several neighbors' complaints, the Metropolitan School Board has allowed Say No to Drugs (SND) baseball games to be played at Urban High on Tuesday and Thursday from 8 p.m. to midnight. The School Board has supported the SND program because it is a successful, nationally recognized program aimed at local drug users and because Urban High's field is the only lighted baseball field within a ten-mile radius of Urban High.

1.   The topic sentence in the original is "Even though the more current cases adopt a liberal reading, there are cases that support a motion to quash service." Presumably, the opening clause is a transition from the preceding discussion. The main clause, "there are cases that support a motion to quash service," is weak. All it says are that the cases exist; it does not get to the real point, which is in the next sentence.

Possible Revision: Even though the more current cases adopt a liberal reading, cases that support a motion to quash service limit *Rovinski* by recognizing that it is not enough to have actual notice.

2.   The original topic sentence in this paragraph is "In order to use *Frasca* to support our client, we must characterize Ms. Clay-Poole's trips to California as visits." The writer may have correctly stated the point of the paragraph in the topic sentence--the trips to California must be characterized as visits--but she has written a rather weak transition.

Possible Revision: Like Frasca's visits to Pennsylvania, Ms. Clay-Poole's trips to California were also visits. If the real point of the paragraph was that her contacts with the California house were minimal, then the topic sentence should state that point.

Possible Revision: Like the defendant in *Frasca*, Ms. Clay-Poole can argue that her contacts with the California residence were minimal.

3.   The "topic sentence"--the plaintiff will point out the factual differences between our case and *Frasca*--does introduce the paragraph, but that is about it. All it does is state the obvious. The sentence lacks both a transition and a general statement about the point of the paragraph.

Possible Revision: The plaintiff, on the other hand, will try to distinguish *Frasca* by showing that Clay-Poole's contacts with the California house are more extensive than Frasca's contacts with the Pennsylvania house.

4.   The topic sentence--Concerning element number one, was Smith a member of the ADEA protected class at the time of his discharge?--is awkward and unsophisticated. Besides beginning with a dangling modifier, "Concerning element number one," it wastes time by asking an obvious question. Avoid such rhetorical questions in memo writing. A better revision is to begin with the answer to that question.

Possible Revision: Smith satisfies element number one because he was a member of the ADEA protected class. At the time of Smith's discharge, ADEA applied only to individuals who were at least forty years old but less than seventy years old. 29 U.S.C. § 631(a) (1982). Smith was forty-nine years old when he was discharged; therefore, he was within the ADEA protected class.

EXERCISE 22D: TOPIC AND CONCLUDING SENTENCES

The topic sentence is effective because it tells the reader why *Riblet v. Spokane-Portland Cement Co.* is being discussed. Notice how the topic sentence is a generalization which is then supported by the specific facts of the case. The conclusion is effective because it brings the reader back to the topic sentence generalization-- damages for annoyances--but now the discussion has advanced so that the reader knows which annoyances are compensable.

Exercise 22E: Paragraph Blocks

<u>Topic Paragraph</u>	=	"'Actual physical control...public."
Topic Sentence	=	Considering the fact pattern... discussion."
Topic Sentence (introduces paragraph block)	=	"Although the primary issue...analysis."
Topic Sentence	=	"In fact, ... decision."
<u>Topic Paragraph</u>	=	"Although it is ... (1958)."
Topic Sentence	=	"The elements...some clarification."
Topic Sentence	=	"The Montana court ... roadway."
Topic Sentence	=	"The Renko fact pattern ...roadway."
Topic Sentence	=	"Positioning ...flow of traffic)."
Topic Sentence	=	"The Montana court ... dissenting)."
Topic Sentence	=	"Because only ... legal significance."
Topic Sentence	=	"In contrast, ... turned off."
<u>Topic Paragraph</u>	=	"In short, ... to sleep."
Topic Sentence	=	"With regard... apparatus."
Topic Sentence	=	"As a sub-issue ... required."
Topic Sentence	=	"If some form ... (1984."
Topic Sentences	=	"The second question, . . . intent." "Intent... two ways."
Topic Sentence	=	"Recent statutory... reasoning."
Topic Sentence	=	"It does not matter...seat."
Topic Sentence (introduces paragraph block)	=	"The Montana court... intoxicated."
Topic Sentence	=	"Focusing...accidents."

Note that short paragraph blocks (for example, only two paragraphs) are often introduced by just a topic sentence, not a full topic paragraph.

Note that on at least one occasion, two sentences work together to create a "topic sentence."

Notice too that this example shows a <u>nesting</u> of paragraph blocks within paragraph blocks. The first paragraph after the heading "Actual Physical Control" is a topic paragraph for the rest of the discussion section, which is one very large paragraph block. Within that very large block is a large paragraph block that begins with the paragraph "The Renko fact pattern differs in the following respects . . ." and includes the rest of the paragraphs in the discussion section. And within the large paragraph block described in the preceding sentence, there is yet another smaller paragraph block starting with the paragraph "In short, . . ." and including the next four paragraphs!

To see the carefully crafted paragraph structure of the discussion section, then, review the following version, which has Roman numerals, capitals, numbers, and lowercase letters to show the nesting block effect.

<u>Discussion</u>

I.   "Actual physical control" is governed by a statute that states in part: "It is unlawful . . . for any person who is under the influence of alcohol to . . . be in actual physical control of a motor vehicle upon the ways of this state open to the public." Mont. Code Ann. §61.8.4011)(a) (1983). Generally, three elements of the statute bear examination: 1) the person must be under the influence of alcohol; 2) the person must be in actual physical control of a motor vehicle; and 3) the motor vehicle must be on the ways of Montana that are open to the public.

<u>Under the Influence</u>

A.   Considering the fact pattern of the Renko case, the court will probably find that the question of whether Mr. Renko was under the influence of alcohol is not worthy of in-depth discussion. The results of the breathalyzer test, the vomit, and the testimony of the arresting officer establish that our client was legally intoxicated at the time of arrest, so the first element of the offense is not at issue.

<u>Ways of the State</u>

B.   Although the primary issue of the case focuses upon resolving questions pertaining to actual physical control, the issue of whether Mr. Renko's truck was on the ways of the state open to the public deserves brief analysis. The traffic code states that "'ways of the state open to the

A-5

public' means any highway, road, alley lane, parking area, or other public or private place adapted and fitted for public travel that is in common use by the public." Mont. Code Ann. § 61.8.101(1)(1983). The language specifically states "adapted and fitted for public travel." Since Mr. Renko's truck was found on the shoulder, the court would have to determine whether the shoulder of a highway is adapted and fitted for public travel. In defining other statutory language, the Montana Supreme Court resorted to dictionary definitions. Webster defines shoulder as "either edge of a roadway: specifically: the part of the roadway *outside the traveled way*" (emphasis added). It is possible, then, that the court could interpret the statutory language narrowly and conclude that the term "ways" does not encompass shoulders.

However, a narrow construction of the term "ways" is unlikely. In fact, there are two strong indications that Montana will favor a broad construction: 1) an extension stated in the statutory definition of "highway"; and 2) an interpretation of "ways" given in a Montana Supreme Court decision. By statutory definition, "[h]ighway means the entire width between the boundary lines of every publicly maintained way when any part thereof is open to the use of the public for purposes of vehicular travel, *except that for the purpose of chapter 8 the term also includes ways which have been or shall be dedicated to public use*." (emphasis added) Mont. Code Ann. ù 61.1.201 (1983). Chapter 8 includes offenses committed while under the influence of alcohol. Since the legislature expanded the statutory definition for alcohol-related offenses, it follows that the legislature intended to broaden, not narrow, the term. Following the legislature's lead, the Montana Supreme Court stipulated that "ways" encompasses state and county right-of-ways, including borrow pits, which road maintenance crews use as sources of dirt and gravel. *State v. Taylor,* 242 Mont. 43, 44, 661 P.2d 33, 34 (1983). It is highly unlikely that the court would include borrow pits but exempt shoulders from the term "ways." The court will probably conclude that Mr. Renko's truck was on the ways of the state open to the public.

<u>Actual Physical Control</u>

C.   Although it is relatively easy to determine that the facts in this case satisfy the elements of "under the influence" and "on the ways," it is more difficult to decide whether they constitute "actual physical control" of a motor vehicle. The statute does not further explain "actual physical control," but the Montana Supreme Court supplied the following dictionary definition: "[I]t means existing or present bodily restraint, directing influence, domination or regulation of an automobile." *State v.Ruona*, 133 Mont. 243, 246, 321 P.2d 615, 618 (1958).

The elements of the definition have not been completely defined; however, the court has given some clarification. In *Ruona*, the court stated that "restraint" includes preventing a car from moving: movement of a vehicle is not necessary for actual physical control. 133 Mont. at 246, 321 P.2d at 618. The court further clarified the term "regulation" by asserting that a sleeping driver who remains behind the steering wheel of a vehicle "remains in a position to regulate" the vehicle and "has not relinquished control" of the vehicle. *Taylor*, 242 Mont. at 44, 661 P.2d 34. Regulation or control is not diminished by the fact that a vehicle is incapable of moving because, as previously noted, movement is not required. *Taylor*, 242 Mont. at 44, 661 P.2d at 34 (citing *Ruona*, 133 Mont. at 247, 321 P.2d at 619).

The Montana court has applied these definitions to cases with the following fact patterns: 1) the driver was asleep and intoxicated; 2) the driver was positioned behind the steering wheel of the motor vehicle; 3) the vehicle's motor was running; 4) the vehicle was parked; and 5) the vehicle was at least partially on the pavement of a roadway. In both of the leading Montana cases, the court held that the driver was in actual physical control of his vehicle. *Ruona*, 133 Mont. 243, 321 P.2d 615; *Taylor*, 242 Mont. 43, 661 P.2d 33. However, the court has not addressed the exact fact pattern presented by the Renko case.

The Renko fact pattern differs in the following respects: 1) the driver was not seated behind the steering wheel; 2) the engine of the vehicle was not running; and 3) the vehicle was not even partially on the traveled portion of the roadway. Although the "driver's position" may be considered separately, "engine not running" and "vehicle not on roadway" are closely related in terms of legal significance and should be analyzed together. In fact, the interrelationship of all three factors should be considered for two reasons. First, although a single factor may not affect the outcome of a case, the combination of that factor with others may be legally significant. Second, the combination of the aforementioned factors may be important in showing the defendant's intent.

    1.   Positioning in the driver's seat is a common element in all the national cases that have found actual physical control of a motionless vehicle, *State v.Smelter*, 36 Wash. App. 439, 441, 674 P.2d 690, 692 (1984), except for one Oklahoma case, *Hughes v. State*, 509 Okla. 157, 535 P.2d 1023 (1975) (defendant was lying across the front seat but was awake and the vehicle was not only on the roadway but also at a 90 degree angle to the flow of traffic). The theory behind the decisions is that an intoxicated person who is seated behind the steering wheel is still in a position to control the vehicle and could be considered a potential threat to the public. *Ruona*, 133 Mont. at 243, 321 P.2d at 619 (quoting *State v. Webb*, 78 Ariz. 8, 274 P.2d 338, (1954)).

The Montana court could view the positioning question in two ways: 1) it could hold that positioning behind the steering wheel is essential to manifest control of the vehicle, *Cincinnati v. Kelley*, 47 Ohio St. 2d 94, 351 N.E.2d 85 (1976); or 2) it could find that positioning is relatively unimportant because once awakened, a driver could quickly move behind the wheel and would pose as great a threat to society as the driver who remained behind the wheel while he slept. *State v. Bugger,* 25 Utah 2d 404, 483 P.2d 442, (1971) (Ellett, J., dissenting). Considering that the Montana court has focused on the idea that the purpose of the statute is to protect the public and has found that a sleeping, intoxicated driver is still a threat to the public, *Ruona,* 133 Mont. at 243, 321 P.2d at 619, the court would probably find that a sleeping, intoxicated driver who is lying on the front seat poses a potential threat to the public.

> 2. Because only a few cases have addressed the issues of whether actual physical control of a vehicle can be established when the engine is not running or when the vehicle is entirely off the traveled portion of the roadway, it is difficult to isolate these factors in terms of legal significance.
>
>   Actual physical control has been found when the vehicle was legally parked and the engine was not running but when the driver was awake and in the driver's seat. *Kelley,* 47 Ohio St. 2d 94, 351 N.E.2d 85. In *Kelley,* the court noted that the defendant was behind the wheel, had possession of the key, and was in such a condition that he could have started the vehicle. 47 Ohio St. 2d 94, 351 N.E.2d 85.

In contrast, courts have been reluctant to find actual physical control when the driver has been found asleep in a vehicle that was legally parked on the shoulder of the roadway with the engine turned off. For example, in *State v. Bugger,* the Utah Supreme Court held that a defendant was not in actual physical control because he was not controlling the vehicle or exercising any dominion over it. *State v. Bugger,* 25 Utah 2d 404, 483 P.2d 442. In *State v. Zavala,* the Arizona Supreme Court held that a defendant had voluntarily relinquished control of the vehicle. *State v. Zavala,* 136 Ariz. 356, 666 P.2d 456, (1983). The Arizona court considered the voluntary action or intent of the driver important and wished to foster the policy of encouraging drunk drivers to pull out of traffic, to turn off the engine, and to go to sleep. *Zavala,* 136 Ariz. 356, 666 P.2d 456, (1983).

In short, before the Montana court can determine whether Mr. Renko was in actual physical control of the vehicle, the court must determine the following issues: 1) whether Mr. Renko had relinquished control of the vehicle; and 2) whether the Montana legislature intended to foster a policy of encouraging intoxicated drivers to pull off the road to sleep.

> > a. With regard to the first issue, other jurisdictions have partially defined "control" and "operate" in terms of the defendant's manipulation of mechanical or electrical apparatus. Cases that relate to such a definition have dealt with defendants who were awake and were attempting either

to brake or to steer inoperable vehicles. *State v. Swift*, 125 Conn. 399, 6 A.2d 359 (1939); *State v.Storrs*, 105 Vt. 180, 163 A. 560 (1933). However, it is conceivable that a court, particularly one that is inclined to broadly construe traffic regulations concerning intoxicated drivers, could apply the "manipulation of mechanical and electrical apparatus" definition in the Renko case. The court could conclude that Mr. Renko's left foot was manipulating the brake pedal and illuminating the brake lights; therefore, he had not relinquished control of the vehicle. The court could reach the same conclusion by finding that Mr. Renko was using "present bodily restraint" to prevent the car from moving.

As a sub-issue in determining control, the court would have to address the question of whether operability is required. If it is not required, then no further discussion of this issue would be necessary; and in light of the Montana court's holding in *Taylor*, operability probably would not be required because movement is not required and the driver was still considered to be in actual physical control of a vehicle that he could not move. 242 Mont. at 43, 661 P.2d at 34.

If some form of operability is required, then the court must decide whether to focus on the defendant's ability to operate the vehicle or on the vehicle's condition. *State v. Smelter*, 36 Wash. App. 439, 444, 674 P.2d 690, 693 (1984). In focusing on the defendant's condition, the court could find that since the defendant had the key and was in the cab of the truck, he would have been able to operate the vehicle had he been awakened. Not only is it possible that he could have operated the truck, it is evident that he did drive the truck from the tavern to the freeway before parking it on the shoulder. In focusing on the vehicle's condition, the Washington court used the trial court's "reasonably operable" standard and defined that term as any malfunction short of a cracked block or a similar problem that would render the vehicle totally inoperable. *Smelter*, 36 Wash. App. at 444, 674 P.2d at 693. By that definition, Mr. Renko's truck was reasonably operable regardless of whether it would start. Therefore, if the Montana court considers operability an issue, it would probably find that Mr. Renko was capable of operating the vehicle and that the vehicle was in reasonably operable condition.

> b. The second question, whether the legislature   wishes to
> foster a policy of encouraging intoxicated drivers to pull off the road to sleep, includes considering the importance of the defendant's intent. Intent and policy can be looked at in two ways. The first, that presented by the Arizona court in *Zavala*, is that the driver who realizes that he is not in condition to drive and pulls off the roadway to sleep should be rewarded. If the court were not to reward such behavior, then the driver would be tempted to proceed to his

destination and would present a greater threat to public safety. 36 Ariz. 356, 666 P.2d 456. The second view is that the drunken driver not only intended to drive but also did drive his car from the tavern to the freeway, and it is better policy to encourage an intoxicated person to avoid driving in the first place. In accord with this view, the Washington court noted that statutes prohibiting driving while intoxicated are primarily preventive measures that are designed to deter intoxicated persons from entering vehicles except as passengers. *Smelter*, 36 Wash. App. at 444, 674 P.2d at 693 (citing *State v. Ghylin*, 250 N.W.2d 252, 255 (N.D. 1977)). The *Smelter* court agreed with other courts that have held that such legislation should be liberally interpreted with the effect of promoting the public interest at the expense of the private interest of the inebriated driver. 36 Wash. App. at 444, 674 P.2d at 693.

Recent statutory revisions in Montana seem to follow this line of reasoning. The Montana legislature revised the traffic code in 1983 and purposely broadened the scope of the laws relating to drunken drivers. The intent was to allow patrol officers to apprehend drunken drivers before such drivers could create accidents. *Montana's Legislative Attempt to Deal with the Drinking Driver: The 1983 DWI Statutes*, 46 Mont. L.Rev. 315 (1985). The Montana court followed suit in *Taylor* by liberally construing the statutes. 242 Mont. 43, 661 P.2d 33. Considering the legislative intent and the court's demonstrated tendencies toward liberal construction, the court will probably side with Justice Ellett, who dissented in *Bugger:*

It does not matter whether the motor is running or is idle nor whether the drunk is in the front seat or in the back seat. His potentiality for harm is lessened but not obviated by a silent motor or a backseat position-- provided, of course, that he is the one in control of the car. It only takes a flick of the wrist to start the motor or to engage the gears, and it requires only a moment of time to get under the wheel from the back seat. A drunk in control of a motor vehicle has such a propensity to cause harm that the statute intended to make it criminal for him to be in a position to do so. *State v. Bugger*, 25 Utah 2d 404, 405, 483 P.2d 442, 443 (1971) (Ellett, J., dissenting).

Conclusion

II.   The Montana court will probably find that Andrew Renko was in actual physical control of a motor vehicle while intoxicated. Although it would be unprecedented to find "actual physical control" when the person was asleep across the front seat and the engine was not running, the Montana court has not been reluctant to break new ground.

The court was a leader in defining "actual physical control," and many jurisdictions have followed the Montana definition.

Focusing on the threat to the public, the Montana legislature broadened the statutes to make it easier to apprehend intoxicated individuals before they cause motor vehicle accidents. The Montana court followed suit by broadly construing statutory wording. The tendency in Montana is toward an expanded definition. Therefore, it would be inconsistent for the court to conclude that Mr. Renko was not in actual physical control of his vehicle.

EXERCISE 22F: PARAGRAPH BLOCKS

Concluding Sentence	=	"The results . . . not at issue."
Concluding Sentence	=	"It is possible . . . shoulders."
Concluding Sentence (for paragraph block)	=	"The court will . . . public."
Concluding Sentence	=	"The statute . . . (1958)."
Concluding Sentence	=	"Regulation . . . at 619."
Concluding Sentence	=	"However, . . . Renko case."
Concluding Sentences	=	"In fact, . . . reasons."
Concluding Sentence	=	"The theory . . . 1954)." "First....Second....intent"
Concluding Sentence	=	"Considering . . . to the public."
Concluding Sentences	=	"The court could conclude...The court could reach...moving."
Concluding Sentence	=	"If it is not...at 34."
Concluding Sentence	=	"Therefore, ... operable condition."
Concluding Sentence	=	"The *Smelter* court . . . at 693."
Concluding Sentence	=	"Considering . . . in *Bugger*."
Concluding Paragraph	=	"It does not matter . . . dissenting."
Concluding Sentence	=	"The court was a leader . . . definition."
Concluding Sentence	=	"Therefore, . . . vehicle."

Note that many paragraphs do not have explicit concluding sentences.

EXERCISE 22G: PARAGRAPH BLOCKS

Different readers will have different opinions about whether the paragraphs are too long or too short in the example. Most readers find the one-sentence paragraph ("In short, ...) effective because it introduce a paragraph block and even though it is only one sentence, it is a rather long sentence with two distinct parts.

Chapter 23
Connections Between Sentences

---

1.   for one year. Recently, Mr. Hillary has been annoyed . . . .

2.   requirements. Therefore, he
      or
      requirements; therefore,

3.   Hillary will further (also) claim that he is specially injured . . . .

4.   (1964). Consequently, the fact that . . . .

5.   (1956). Moreover, the use . . . .

6.   (1930). Similarly, Hillary . . . .

7.   subjective values. Rather, the presence of . . . .

8.   public nuisance. He could, however, consider . . . .

9.   compelling. First, the noise . . . "ordinary." *Hayes*, 311. Second, it . . . manner."
      Id. Third, no intoxicants . . . beach. *Id.* at 313. Fourth, the activities . . . .

10.   recreation.   In addition, the court found . . . .

1.   For this information, the Justice Department offered him a reward.

2.   His only motive for assisting the Justice Department was to receive a reward.

3.   These actions (or These operational actions) do not include discretionary,
      planning, or design actions.

4.   These acts are performed by agents who do not exercise their own judgment.
      or
      The agents perform these acts without exercising their own judgment.

5. Because of these records, the IRS examined Mr. Snowadzki's tax returns . . . .
   or
   These records prompted the IRS to examine . . . .

EXERCISE 23C: DOVETAILING

1. The impact of the cars threw Mrs. White against . . . .
   As a result of the accident, she gave birth . . . .
   Because of the loss of this child, she is suffering . . . .

2. Such evidence might include injuries incurred by plaintiffs in similar situations.
   Using this evidence, a jury would determine . . . .

3. After conferring with panel members and considering their report, the Governor,
   by Executive Order, initiated a daycare facility program inspection . . . . The
   memorandum directed the inspectors to consider seven factors.

Chapter 24
Effective Sentences

EXERCISE 24A: ACTIVE AND PASSIVE VOICE

1. S = plaintiff V = accepted O = offer   ACTIVE

2. S = (Texas) law V = requires O = balancing   ACTIVE

3. S = term V = will be defined   PASSIVE

4. S = court V = has followed   O = trend ACTIVE

5. S = case V = may be strengthened   PASSIVE

6. S = (prescriptive) easement V = had been established PASSIVE

7. S = (objective) acts V = had established O = (prescriptive) easement   ACTIVE

8. S = right V = can be revoked   PASSIVE

9. S = Mrs. Townsend V = can revoke O = right   ACTIVE

10. S = interpretation V = has been left   PASSIVE

This sentence is the most difficult in the exercise. It is passive voice because the interpretation is not doing the "has been left"; rather, "has been left" has been done to the interpretation. The real doer of the action "has been left" is hard to pinpoint because it is our system of laws and government that has us leave interpretation of rules up to the courts.

EXERCISE 24B: PASSIVE VOICE

1. Clyde Pearson <u>owns</u> Pearson & Sons Lawn Service.

2. After Officer O'Neill <u>found</u> Mr. Lee's truck in the ditch, Officer O'Neill <u>called</u> for an ambulance.

3. The Montana court <u>focused</u> on the idea that the legislature <u>intended</u> to prevent the dumping of toxic waste.

4. Although the police <u>did not find</u> the marijuana in the bedroom, Officer Miller <u>found</u> a film canister filled with cocaine.

5.   The Fourth Amendment <u>stipulates</u> important particularities: the warrant <u>must state</u> the place to be searched and the things to be seized.

6.   The <u>Anderson</u> court's language <u>supports</u> Fremont's argument that the broad scope of the search <u>violated</u> his right to privacy.

7.   Apparently Tom <u>had driven</u> the business car on prior occasions, but his father <u>did not give</u> him specific permission to drive the business car on the day of the accident.

8.   The courts <u>have</u> not <u>ruled</u> on the question of whether a non-viable fetus is a minor child; however, the courts <u>recognize</u> the rights of non-viable fetuses in other areas of the law.

9.   The Wilsons <u>should recover</u> the fair market value of the tractor because Washington tort law <u>provides</u> for the recovery of fair market value of property that has been destroyed.

10. Statutory law <u>defines</u> private nuisance as "everything not included as a public nuisance."

EXERCISE 24C: PASSIVE VOICE

1.   E   The person or thing performing the action is relatively unimportant.

2.   E   The subject "such arrangements" of the passive voice verb provides a strong link between the subordinate clause and the main clause.

3.   I   Active voice is more concise. Revise to "For the next ten years, all the landowners used the easement." (11 words in revision vs. 13 words in original)

     or

     E   In a context in which the focus of the writing was on the easement itself and not the landowners who used it, then the original sentence would be effective.

4. E Passive voice in the clause allows the writer to place the connecting idea, the description of the assailant, at the end of the sentence where it can lead into the subsequent sentence about the defendant's description. Passive voice is also more effective for the defendant because it downplays the doer of the action. Although a plaintiff's brief probably would not use the facts from these two sentences in this form, the active voice version-- "a white male with blue eyes and blond hair assaulted her"--would be more effective for the plaintiff.

5. E If the victim did not see her assailant, the person or thing performing the action is unknown. Again, the passive is more effective for the defendant.

    or

    I In a plaintiff's brief, the writer would want to use active voice and include the doer of the action if that person or thing is known: "Testimony from the attending physician corroborates the victim's testimony that the defendant struck her from behind."

6. E Passive voice in the first sentence moves the connecting idea, "Cathy Nock," to the end position. The second sentence begins with the connecting idea, "Ms. Nock."

7. E Person or thing performing the action is unknown or relatively unimportant.

8. E It is probably undesirable to disclose the identity of the person performing the action, or that person may be unknown. In a defendant's brief, the use of the passive voice is more effective. In a plaintiff's brief the active voice would be more effective, particularly if the doer of the action is known.

9. I Active voice is more concise. Revise to "Both parties signed a standard form contract that detailed the terms of the agreement." (Fourteen words in revision vs. sixteen words in original.) Passive voice in original also separates subject from verb. (See Section D of this chapter.)

    or

    E However, in a context in which the focus of the writing is on the standard form contract, the passive voice may be more effective.

10. E Person or thing performing the action is relatively unimportant.

1.   S = It V = could be argued. Revision: The defense could argue that Mr. Smith was out of the state at the time of the robbery.

2.   S = It V = is. Revision: Both parties intended to enter into a contract

3.   S = It V = is. Revision: A fair market value probably does not exist for the poem.

4.   S = endorsement V = is required. The check must be endorsed before the funds can be transferred.

or

The bank requires that the check be endorsed before the funds are transferred.

or

You must endorse the check before the funds can be transferred. Notice that you can have a concrete subject with either an active or passive voice verb.

5.   S = It V = would appear. Revision: Apparently, our request will be granted.

or

Apparently, the court will grant our request. Notice that you can have a concrete subject with either an active or passive voice verb.

6.   S = confirmation V = is required. Congress must confirm all federal judicial appointments.

7.   S = It V = is. Revision: The defendant was refused admission to medical school because of his criminal record.

8.   S = aspect V = is. Revision: Mr. Nolan's fingerprints on the knife will be difficult to discount.

9.   S = It V = should be pointed out. Revision: South Land Timber's shipments to all three customers were consistently late.

or

Add the person or thing doing the action "The prosecution should point out that . . . ."

10.   S = factor V = caused. Revision: The defendant's earlier perjury conviction
         caused the jury to discount her testimony in this case.

or

The jury discounted the defendant's testimony in this case because she had an
earlier perjury conviction.

EXERCISE 24E: ACTION VERBS

1.   S = way V = is. Revised: A court determines mutual assent by looking at the
         objective manifestations of the parties' actions.

2.   S = governor V = made. Revised: The governor stated that he would not testify
         for the defense.

3.   S = jury V = had. Revised: The jury knew about (of) the defendant's prior
         record.

4.   S = facts V = are. Revised: That witness must confirm several facts.

5.   S = *Hanford v. Goehry* V = concerned. Revised: In *Hanford v. Goehry*, a car
         was kept at the father's place of business.

6.   S = nurse V = made. Revised: The nurse attempted to disconnect the life
         support system.

7.   S = holding V = makes. Revised: The *Harbeson* court suggested that the
         Florida courts are moving towards compensation for loss without applying the
         old standards.

8.   S = instances V = were. Revised: The Parkers never asserted their rights
         against the Lindquists.

9.   S = *State v. Hughes* V = involved. Revised: In *State v. Hughes*, a defendant
         shot two police officers while resisting arrest for another murder.

10.   S = heirs V = are. Revised: The two heirs disagree over the division of
         property.

1. S = contract V = was signed. Revised: Both parties signed a standard form contract that detailed all the terms of the agreement except for the shipper's liability.

2. S = Goods V = must have. Revised: The transaction must be in writing for the sale of goods over five hundred dollars ($500.00).

3. S = possibility V = is. Revised: The legislature revised the statute because it recognized the possibility that an intoxicated driver may decide to continue driving rather than be arrested after pulling over to the shoulder of the road.

4. S =theory V = is. Revised: The "moral right doctrine" is another theory available to Mr. Henderson but not to his co-defendants.

5. From Lloyd's statement to his tax preparer that "the lunches were really social," we can infer that Lloyd intentionally misrepresented at least some of the information.

    or

    Lloyd told his tax preparer that "the lunches were really social." That statement indicates that Lloyd intentionally misrepresented at least some of the information. (Some readers may not object to the original sentence because the quoted material helps to set off some of the intervening words.)

6. S = reading V = favored. Revised: Despite its insistence that there was no accompanying oral agreement, the court read the written contract in a light most favorable to the tire manufacturer.

7. S = court V = stated. Revised: In another case involving the revision of a law manual, the court stated that "the purchase of a copyright did not carry with it a license to defame . . . ."

8. S = name and reputation   V = have been injured. Revised: The libelous conduct of *Trade Union World* has injured our client's name and reputation as an upstanding citizen and honest businessman who treats his employees fairly.

9. S = concept V = suggests. Revised: When applied to the present case, the concept of voluntary assumption of duty suggests that the State voluntarily assumed a duty to use due care in conducting inspections of nursing homes. (Also consider omitting "the concept of.")

10. S = argument V = is. Revised: The State may argue that it owes a duty only to the public generally and not to any individual, but such an argument is not persuasive.
     (Some readers may not object to the original sentence with the subject and verb far apart.)

Exercise 24G: Subject-Verb Review

1. S-V distance; weak verb: action is buried in the noun "research."
    Revised: I have researched your potential claim . . .

    or

    I have fully researched your potential claim . . . .

    or

    I have completed my research on your claim . . . .

2. weak subject: too abstract; weak verb: form of "to be."
    Revised: My opinion is based on the current statutory provisions . . . . (This revision is an effective use of passive voice.)

    or

    I base my opinion on the current statutory provisions.

3. ineffective passive.
    Revised: You terminated that lease . . . .

4. ineffective passive. Note the compound verb
    Revised: He received this notice of termination with at least 30 days' notice and accepted it as valid.

5. weak verbs: form of "to be." Note the compound verb.
    Revised: As of September 10, 2009, you have not been reimbursed your $800.00 security deposit, nor have you received any written explanation from your former landlord telling why he has not returned the money. (This revision is an effective use of passive voice.)

    or

    As of September 10, 2009, your landlord has neither reimbursed your $800.00

security deposit nor sent you a written explanation of why he has not returned the money.

6.   ineffective passive; S-V distance.
      Revised: . . . you have sent four letters to Mr. Printer inquiring about your deposit.

7.   ineffective passive.
      Revised: You left the apartment clean and undamaged.

8.   weak verb; S-V distance.
      Revised: Under the relevant Iowa statute, you have a strong chance of recovering your deposit.

9.   weak verb: form of "to be"; action buried in noun "requirement."
      Revised: Generally, the law requires that landlords. . . .

10.   passive.
      Revised: Since Mr. Printer sent no refund or statement . . . .

EXERCISE 24H: SENTENCE LENGTH

1.   Traditionally, Florida courts have deferred to the legislature's policy judgment on the propriety of punitive damages award. They have manifested this deference by adhering rigidly to the rule that punitive damages should be awarded with the greatest caution and only where specifically authorized by statute.

2.   In determining whether a private citizen is an instrument or agent of the government, the court will examine two critical factors: (1) the government's knowledge or acquiescence and (2) the intent of the party performing the search.

3.   Infringement is an interference with the rights granted to another under a law, a regulation, or a contract. It is usually categorized as infringement of copyright, infringement of patents, or infringement of trademarks.

      or

      Infringement comprises three categories: infringement of copyrights, of patents, and of trademarks.

4. In *Board of Regents*, the court held that the trial court correctly withheld a jury instruction regarding arson from the jury. The court reasoned that the theory of arson was only a mere possibility and did not rise above speculation and conjecture.

5. In *E. I. duPont de Nemorus & Co., Inc. v. Christopher,* the defendants used an airplane to photograph the plaintiff's Beaumont, Texas plant. The plant contained, in an open area, a secret but thus far unpatented process for producing methanol. The process had been developed by duPont at considerable time and expense, and it had provided duPont with a significant advantage over its competitors.

6. The insurance adjustor testified that the defendant's brakes were not functioning properly. He based his conclusion upon a physical inspection of the accident area for skid marks both the night of the accident and the next day during daylight. He found one distinct skid mark and one virtually non-existent skid mark.

7. Under a negligence per se or common law theory of negligence, is a tavern owner liable when he served alcohol to a minor without checking her identification, when he continued to serve her alcohol after she spilled a drink and sang while on top of a table, and when the car she was driving later collided with another vehicle, causing personal injury.

8. The plaintiff may obtain a summary of facts known and opinions held by the nontestifying expert by other means: through depositions of occupants of the cars or through another expert evaluating the facts and making a conclusion.

9. Under N.Y. Penal Law §125.25(3) (McKinney 1975), the felony murder rule, would a charge of second degree murder be valid when the defendant was one of three participants in a robbery, when the store owner had a previous heart condition, when the store owner subsequently died of a massive heart attack, and when his physician states that the stress of the robbery undoubtedly caused the heart attack.

10. Regardless of the victim's previous heart condition and the foreseeability of his death, the felony-murder rule applies for two reasons: 1) robbery is inherently dangerous and 2) a nexus has been established between the robbery and homicide.

EXERCISE 24I: SENTENCE LENGTH

Sentence one of paragraph one can be trimmed from 58 words to 31 words by eliminating unnecessary wordiness. Some writers may prefer to retain the date in the introductory phrase; others prefer to omit it because it is included in the citation.

Revised:

The Equal Credit Opportunity Act (ECOA) was enacted to ensure that all firms that extend credit make that credit equally available to creditworthy customers without regard to sex or marital status. (31 words)

Sentence two of paragraph one is somewhat long at 37 words. Although the commas separating the items in the series help to break up the sentence a bit, a colon provides a strong break between the first half of the sentence and the possible reasons for credit discrimination. Again, the date is included in the citation.

Revised:

The ECOA was later expanded to prohibit credit discrimination for the following reasons: (13 words) race, color, national origin, age, receipt of public assistance income, or the exercise in good faith of the rights guaranteed under the Consumer Credit Protection Act. (26 words).

Sentence three of paragraph two, originally a 40 word sentence, can be broken up into three shorter sentences.

Revised:

The ECOA was enacted as both a consumer protection statute and an antidiscrimination statute. (14 words) As a consumer protection statute, the ECOA was designed to provide accurate information to and about consumers involved in credit transactions. (21 words) As an antidiscrimination statute, the ECOA was designed to shield protected classes of consumers from credit discrimination. (17 words)

EXERCISE 24J: SENTENCES REVIEW

1. None of the sentences are overly long (22-10-33-16 words, respectively), and there seems to be sufficient variety in the sentence length. The one short sentence, however, emphasizes a point unfavorable to the client.

   Revised:

   Mr. Barker is a stable, loving father, who will provide a stimulating home environment for the Barkers' two children, George and Karen. Although the psychiatrist's report suggests that Mr. Barker may be compulsive, this trait is not unusual for highly successful businessmen. In fact, Mr. Barker's success in business gives him more flexibility in his work schedule. Consequently, he will have even more time for his children. Furthermore, the psychologist's report agrees that Mr. Barker has potential to be a sensitive, outgoing parent.

2.   None of the sentences are overly long (9-13-15-17 words, respectively), but they lack sufficient variety in sentence length to be interesting.

Revised:

Mrs. Barker's psychological stability, however, is far from certain. She has been diagnosed as having histrionic tendencies and as being mildly hysterical, two disorders which, according to her psychologist, make her prone to alcohol and chemical dependency. Once, this dependency became so severe that Mrs. Barker required medical care to cope with her alcoholism.

EXERCISE 24K: SENTENCES REVIEW

The Franklins immediately paid the construction and engineering costs and sought reimbursement from the Morgans. The Morgans refused payment, contending that the Franklins accepted the premises "as is." The Morgans further contended that, although the bracing was required on a part of the structure specifically reserved to the Morgans, the bracing was not a repair.

At the time of the arbitration, the Franklins are seeking recovery from the Morgans for the amount to repair the exterior wall; the Morgans are seeking a judgment declaring that they are not responsible for the repair costs.

EXERCISE 24L: EMPHASIS

1.   When the police officers found her, the girl was wearing only her shoes and she was tied to a tree.

2.   When the police officers found her, the girl was tied to a tree and wearing only one item of clothing: her shoes.

3.   Seven people were killed on July 14, 1986, in a nuclear accident at Beatty, Nevada -- the first fatal accident at the Nevada site.

or

The first fatal nuclear accident at the Beatty, Nevada site occurred on July 14, 1986, killing seven people.

4.   If the defendant is convicted of this offense, a judge has the option of imposing a fine not to exceed $5,000 and sentencing him to period of two to ten years.

5.   The plaintiff's final argument will depend on whether he can prove a substantial depreciation -- over $20,000 -- of the value of his property.

     or

     The plaintiff's final argument will depend on whether he can prove a depreciation of his property value of over $20,000.

6.   Under the Uniform Building Code, the tenant has no maintenance obligations; the obligation to maintain the building falls on the owner.

7.   Under the Uniform Building Code, the obligation to maintain the building falls on the owner, not the tenant.

8.   We can prove that the dog is vicious: he has bitten three people.

9.   The church freely admits that it operated a fulltime school without a special use permit.

10. The church operated a fulltime school without a special use permit--a point the church admits freely.

EXERCISE 24M: SINGLE WORD EMPHASIZERS

1.   Although five witnesses have placed Sharon Clark at the scene of the crime, she still claims she was at home alone.

2.   An explosives expert testified that any slight change in the cabin pressure would activate the detonator.

3.   According to company regulations, no employee could leave his or her post until the supervisor on duty had assigned a replacement.

4.   In the union's history, an allegation of this severity has never been made.

     or

     Never before in the union's history has an allegation of this severity been made.

5.   It was the deceased, not the defendant, who ran the stoplight.

6.   All the bonds in the safety deposit box were under her name.

7.   The bonds in the safety deposit box were under only her name.

        or

        Only the bonds in the safety deposit box were under her name.

8.   Every member of the union voted to ratify the contract.

9.   Despite numerous warnings from the Environmental Protection Agency, National Chemical still disposed of waste by-products by dumping them in the bay.

10.   Laura Smith died, not from the operation, but from inadequate post operative care.

EXERCISE 24N: CHANGING WORD ORDER

1.   In a lineup with no other bearded men, the defendant was later identified.

2.   The defendant--at gunpoint--forced Ms. Harper to perform fellatio.

3.   The starter's pistol has been identified by two witnesses as the weapon used.

4.   Only for a manifest abuse will the trial court's exercise of this discretion be overturned on appeal.

5.   The burden of proof mere assertions do not satisfy.

6.   The defendant could have effectively corrected, at the time they were made, all alleged errors.

7.   On each separate count, the State had strong evidence.

8.   The words "pistol" and "revolver" are included in the definition of deadly weapon.

9.   Also denied was the defendant's motion to sever Counts I and II from Counts III, IV, and V.

10.   On all five counts, the defendant was convicted by the jury.

1. Mr. Baylor's behavior shows a clear pattern: first, intimidating his children; then, intimidating his wife; and now, intimidating a witness.

2. Thomas Dever was not insane when he threatened Miss Dever in October. He was not insane when he shadowed her for two weeks in November. And he was not insane when he brutally killed her on Christmas Eve.

3. We want to believe that our country acted fairly. We want to believe that our country acted wisely. We do not want to believe that our country acted maliciously.

4. After twenty years in prison, Carl Wilson returned to society without a job, without a home, without a cent in the bank.

    or

    . . . with no job, with no home, and with no money in the bank.

5. All the opposition lacks is proof: proof that the defendant was at the scene of the crime, proof that the defendant had a motive, and proof that the defendant committed the deed.

6. No court, no jury, and no jail term will undo what Frank Morris has done.

7. Desmond Adams rebuilt his business with his own money, with his own hard work, and without the help of his former partner.

8. It was Judith Davis, not Martin Davis, who refused to see a marriage counselor. It was Judith Davis, not Martin Davis, who filed for a divorce. And now it is Judith Davis, not Martin Davis, who wants an even larger share of her husband's pension.

9. In the contract for the Lowell building, Kyle Davis had a silent partner: Ronald Thomas. In the contract for the Madison complex, Kyle Davis had a silent partner: Ronald Thomas. But in the contract for the Westside shopping mall, Kyle Davis acted alone.

10. With malice aforethought, Michael Mann bought the .38 caliber pistol at Seaside Pawn Shop. With malice aforethought, he waited in the car for Howard Peterson to return home from work. And with malice aforethought, Michael Mann followed Howard Peterson up to his first door and shot him three times in the chest.

Chapter 25
Effective Words

Exercise 25A: Word Choice

1. ~~exhibit~~ indicate, suggest, show, prove, establish
   ~~for~~ of

2. ~~constitute this as~~ determine, hold

3. ~~display~~ show

4. ~~have ... give to~~ order ... for ~~kids~~ children

5. ~~explored to find~~ looked to see ~~to~~ of

6. ~~tough~~ difficult ~~award~~ grant

7. ~~annunciated~~ enunciated

8. ~~ceased~~ was dissolved

9. ~~decreed~~ found (or simply awarded damages) ~~decreed~~ granted

10. ~~set~~ created, established

11. ~~beyond~~ by

12. ~~dissent~~ descent

13. ~~exasperated~~ exacerbated

14. ~~evokes~~ invokes

15. ~~arterial~~ ulterior

Exercise 25B: Consistent Terms

The corrected words are in bold.

     A court will need to examine the tests for two doctrines, *respondeat superior* and "loaned servant," to determine whether Dr. Robinson or Bondurant Temporary Agency, Inc. (Bondurant) can be held vicariously liable for the destruction of Ms. Bakerman's coat. The first doctrine, *respondeat superior*, has a three-prong test. The first two prongs of the test are met. First, Carol Kester was negligent for the destruction of the coat. *See Nyman v. MacRae Bros. Constr. Co.*, 69 Wash. 2d 285, 287, 418 P.2d 253, 254 (1966). Second, Carol was acting within the scope of her employment at the time of the tortious act. *See Kuehn v. White*, 24 Wash. App. 274, 277, 600 P.2d 679, 682 (1979). There will be a dispute about the third **prong**: whether Carol was under the control of Bondurant, her general employer, or under the control of Dr. Robinson, her temporary employer at the time the coat was destroyed. *See Kroshus v. Koury*, 20 Wash. App. 258, 263, 633 P.2d 909, 911 (1981) (quoting *McLean v. St. Regis Paper Co.*, 6 Wash. App. 727, 732, 496 P.2d 571, 574 (1972)).

The second **doctrine**, "loaned servant," has a three-part test to determine who has control of a temporary employee. *Pichler v. Pacific Mechanical Constr.*, 1 Wash App. 447, 450-51, 462 P.2d 960, 963 (1969). The first and second parts of the test — who has the right to select or hire and fire the servant and who has the right to direct how the servant shall perform his duties — will be disputed, but the most important **part** will be who had exclusive control or the right to exclusive control at the time of the tortious act. *Pichler*, 1 Wash. App. at 450-51, 462 P.2d at 963.

Exercise 25C: Appropriate Comparisons

1. The grief over the loss of a six-week-old fetus is hardly comparable to the grief over the loss of a viable fetus.

2. This policy of protecting the **investor** from the various schemes devised by promoters has been a persuasive cornerstone for judicial interpretation of **investment** contracts in the post-*Howey* era. *See, e.g., SEC v. Glenn W. Turner Enter., Inc.*, 474 F.2d 476 (9th Cir. 1973). However, the Ninth Circuit apparently does not find **investor** protection alone determinative when interpreting federal securities law. Other factors may come into play, such as the underlying nature of the financial relationship between the **investor** and the promoter. *See, e.g., Brodt v. Bache & Co., Inc.*, 595 F.2d 459 (9th Cir. 1978). Consequently, legal analysis of CP's **investment** scheme does not yield a precise conclusion about whether a Ninth Circuit federal court would deem it to be an **investment** contract.

3. Correct. A case is compared with a case.

4. A potential plaintiff would argue that the fetus is the personal property of the mother. This argument would be similar to the **argument in** *Moore* in that the body part that was surgically removed was the personal property of the plaintiff patient.

5. In its decision, the *Brodt* court explicitly rejected using the concept of "horizontal commonality" employed in other circuits; that **concept** would require that there be a pooling of interests combined with a pro-rata sharing of profits. *Id.* at 460. Instead, the court used the broader **concept** of "vertical commonality," which requires that the investor and the promoter be involved in some common venture without mandating that other investors also be involved in the venture. *Id.* at 461 (citing *Hector v. Wiens*, 533 F.2d 429 (9th Cir. 1976).

   Note: Although most readers would not have a problem with the synonym "approach," it is more precise to retain the earlier term "concept." "Concept" must replace "principle" so that "horizontal commonality" and "vertical commonality" are properly compared.

Exercise 25D: Subject-Verb-Object Combinations

1.   language has broadened
      [subject]   [verb]

      Revision:
      Since then, the courts' interpretation of the language has broadened.

2.   *Eggert*   says
      [subject]   [verb]

      Revision:
      As for the burden of proof, the *Eggert* court says that the burden is on the plaintiff to establish a right to maintain the action in an action for conversion.

3.   weight (of case law)   would deny   relief
            [subject]   [verb]   [object]

      Revision:
      Should Mr. Robinson bring suit, a court is likely to deny him relief based upon the great weight of the case law.

4.   conviction   has been interpreted
      [subject]   [verb]

      Revision:
      Courts in the Fourth Circuit have interpreted § 1071 as requiring proof of four elements for a conviction: 1) that a federal warrant had been issued for the fugitive's arrest; 2) that the defendant had knowledge that a warrant had been issued for the fugitive's arrest; 3) that the defendant actually harbored or concealed the fugitive; and 4) that defendant intended to prevent the fugitive's discovery or arrest.

5.   (issues) that   argue
      [subject]   [verb]

      Revision:
      There are persuasive arguments based on public policy for restricting a woman's right to fetal tissue.

6.   test   is determined (by the use)
        [subject]   [verb]

        Revision:
        To determine whether a nuisance exists, the court considers the use to which the property is put.

7.   likelihood   is (favorable)
        [subject]   [verb]

        Revision:
        The court is likely to determine that this is an established custodial environment.

8.   doctrine   withheld   property
        [subject] [verb]   [object]

        Revision:
        Under the trust fund doctrine, which was created by the equity courts to protect creditors when an indebted corporation dissolved, the corporation's property was withheld to pay off debts.

9.   New Age Aerobics may (not) be causing hazards . . . congestion . . . buildings
           [subject]   [verb]   [objects]

        Note that the subject and verb must match each of the objects. Can New Age aerobics cause a building?

        Revision:
        Even though New Age Aerobics may not be responsible for safety hazards, increased traffic congestion, or unsightly buildings, the cumulative effects of its activities should be considered.

10.   probability   is (unlikely)
           [subject]   [verb]

        Revision:
        Mrs. Davis probably cannot meet this required standard of proof.

Exercise 25E: Grammatical Ambiguities

See Answer Key for Exercises 27.L, 27.M, 27.N, and 27.O.

1. Two defenses are available to Acme. OR Acme has two available defenses.

2. You are probably bound by the written agreement simply because you signed it.

3. In determining whether there was a sudden emergency, courts also consider whether there was sufficient warning that should have alerted the driver to the imminent danger. (It is effective to keep both *there was* expletives because the point of the sentence is the existence of a sudden emergency and the existence of sufficient warning.)

4. The court will liberally construe Fed. R. Civ. P. 4(d)(1).

5. The court may follow the view that "in a highly mobile and affluent society, it is unrealistic to interpret 4(d)(1) so that the person to be served has only one dwelling house or usual place of abode at which process may be left." 4A Charles Alan Wright & Arthur R. Miller, *Federal Practice and Procedures* § 1096 (2d ed. 1987).

6. The two parties differ over whether the deposit is refundable.

7. The court inferred that because the papers were left with appellant's mother, the appellant received them.

8. If "substantial" is held to be analogous with "principal," then five percent of a total business would be the minimum necessary to establish that certain sales of merchandise are a "principal" part of a business.

9. We could argue that Ms. Fox so conditioned her acceptance of your offer as to create a counteroffer.

10. The legislature intended to encourage corporations to explore new ways of reducing energy costs.

11. After thoroughly researching your complaint against Mr. Brown, I conclude that the best way to recover the $2500 that he owes you is to file a lien against his orchard.

12. The boys deny making any threats.

13. The defendant has moved to suppress the evidence seized after the arrest.

14. The trial court did not err in failing to instruct on the absence of intervening cause.

15. After the court overruled the defense counsel's objection, the witness answered yes.

Exercise 25G: Conciseness

1. Before I can advise you, I need to ask whether your husband knew that his life expectancy was short.

2. In addition to the procedure that begins the process, the plant foreman must then start the back-up system.

3. The night watchman usually ends his rounds at 5 a.m. after inspecting each safe in the building.

4. Before trial, the defendant will file a Motion in Limine to exclude evidence of his prior convictions.

5. The consensus among the board members was that having employees follow a certain procedure when they entered or left the building would not end employee theft.

6. The Parkers assumed that real estate agents who list a home for sale are obligated to appraise that home.

7. For two months during 2009, Mr. Wilson aided a known felon by allowing her to use his cabin to hide from the police.

8. There is no constitutional right to receive credit, but much can be done to insure that credit availability is fair.

9. In my opinion, we cannot get an injunction to eliminate the factory's noon whistle.

10. We ordered the building vacated so that the inhabitants would be safe.

Exercise 25H: Conciseness

1. In late October 1997, Kyle Nelson asked Frances Miles, an acquaintance, to house sit for him while he was away on vacation.

2.   The trial judge calculated O'Hara's offender score as seven, basing her decision on Or. Rev. Stat. § 137.370(4), which states in part that "[u]nless the court expressly orders otherwise, a term of imprisonment shall be concurrent with the remainder of any sentence previously imposed at the time the court imposes sentence."

3.   Instruction 10 did not shift the ultimate burden of proof to Chin, create any mandatory presumption, or impose any burden of producing evidence on Chin. Rather, the instruction states that the presumption "is not binding" upon the jury and that the jury can determine "what weight, if any," to give to the presumption.

4.   At the disposition hearing, the state presented a document describing Ortega's prior criminal history: ten burglary convictions and three minor offenses subject to diversion.

5.   Peters moved to Chesterville to be near her husband, who was an inmate at the state penitentiary at Chesterville. Upon arriving in Chesterville, Peters met a woman whose husband was also an inmate in the penitentiary.

6.   The legislature directed the Department of Ecology to publish a statutorily prescribed notice by four different means: 1) publication of the notice once a year for five years in major as well as local newspapers; 2) publication of the notice every six months on radio and television stations broadcasting in every county; and 3) posting the notice in a conspicuous location in every county; and 4) including a copy of the notice with notices of taxes due for 1972 mailed by each county treasurer.

7.   The Court of Appeals upheld the rape conviction and corresponding habitual criminal finding but reversed the assault conviction.

.   At 2:20 a.m. on September 29, 2008, Brian Smith entered his parents' bedroom where they were sleeping. Brian shot his mother in the head with a 30.06 rifle, killing her. Mr. Smith woke up and saw Brian leave the bedroom. Unable to telephone for help because Brian had taken the telephone off the hook in the kitchen, Mr. Smith locked the bedroom door and escaped through the window. Brian returned to the bedroom, intending to kill his father, but found that he had escaped.

9.   Upon arriving at the scene, the officers discovered Barbara Wilson-Hughes in a comatose condition and immediately called an emergency medical unit. The medical unit transported Mrs. Wilson-Hughes to a local hospital where she was treated for a "closed-head injury" and several facial lacerations.

10.   In *Workman*, the court set forth a two-prong test for determining when lesser offense instructions should be given: 1) each element of the lesser offense must

be a necessary element of the offense charged; 2) evidence must support an inference that the lesser crime was committed.

Exercise 25I: Conciseness Review

1.   Each plaintiff received $20,000 in damages.

2.   A driver who refuses to wear prescription glasses and who drives faster than the speed limit is a hazard.

3.   Trooper Evans, who investigated the accident, testified that the "primary casual factor" of the accident had been the defendant's intoxicated state.

4.   Jones will argue that he did not knowingly and voluntarily consent to Officer Nguyen's search of his wallet. Jones will further argue that the items discovered during the search, particularly the stolen charge card, exceeded the scope of his consent.

5.   Henson responded to the public disclosure request by providing all documents, except two letters, which were excluded because they contained proprietary or private information about Henson's business practices.

6.   Mail was sent to their separate addresses, but on occasion an invitation addressed to both of them would come to Mr. Patel's address.

7.   Mr. McRae stated that he discussed only the manufacture and delivery of the equipment with Jim Drane, the principal of Lakeland Elementary, and reiterated that they did not discuss installation.

8.   Recognizing that in similar cases courts have issued directed verdicts, I expect that you will also get a directed verdict.

9.   The court correctly denied the defendant's motion for a new trial because the defendant must suggest more than a "possibility of prejudice."

10.   Because my client was uninformed about the law and because she is elderly, this court should grant her special consideration. She wants only to give her prized hand-painted china collection to her community library.

1.   "[C]omfortable enjoyment means both mental quiet and physical comfort." *Park v. Stolzheise*, 24 Wash. 2d 781, 167 P.2d 412 (1946). The neighbors will argue that floodlights on until midnight adversely affects their physical comfort because their sleep is disturbed by the lights beaming through the bedroom windows. To support this contention, the neighbors will use *Bruskland* where the court stated that automobile headlights shining upon a bedroom window constituted a private nuisance because they unreasonably interfered with owners' comfortable enjoyment of the property. 42 Wash. 2d at 348. Consequently, the trier of fact will probably rule that the floodlights interfered with the neighbors' comfortable enjoyment of their property.

2.   In addition, the court must determine whether the plaintiff "thrust into the controversy in an attempt to influence the outcome." *Hutchinson*, 443 U.S. at 135. For example, the *Waldbaum* court held that the plaintiff had thrust into a controversy in an attempt to influence its outcome when the plaintiff invited both the press and the public to a special meeting it held to discuss the introduction of unit pricing and open dating into supermarkets.

3.   Although the two levels of immunity have been well defined, the level of immunity that parole board members should be afforded remains unclear. To analyze the case at hand, the court must examine those decisions of the Supreme Court, Third Circuit, and Ninth Circuit concerning the levels of immunity accorded to public officials that present the tests to determine the type and scope of immunity that the Board members should be afforded.

25K: Legalese

Dear Mr. Patterson:

Enclosed is a copy of the Notice of Appeal that was filed with the King County Superior Court on November 25. This notice will be immediately sent to the Court of Appeals.

Because your case involves your constitutional rights, the Court of Appeals will do a *de novo* review of your case; that is, the Court will do a "fresh" review of the entire case as though there had been no trial court decision. Unfortunately, however, we are unlikely to win at appellate court level. As we have discussed before, show-ups are not automatically impermissible. As a result, the Court of Appeals will need, among other things, to balance the suggestiveness of the show-up with the reliability of the identifications. In other words, the appellate court will consider the five factors and probably reach the same conclusion as the trial court.

Even though these cases are rarely reversed on appeal, our firm will exercise the utmost effort on your behalf. If we lose at the appellate level, you can then decide if you want us to file a writ of certiorari on your behalf asking that your case by heard by the Supreme Court.

Very truly yours,

Ms. Sarah Fisher

Exercise 25L: Gender-Neutral Language

1. masked intruder OR masked robber OR masked and armed assailant. (If the person is masked, the sex is probably unknown.)

2. neighbor. (If the wife lives with her husband, she is a neighbor as well.)

3. the human family.

4. Dear Members of the Board
    or
    Dear Board Members.

5. the driver in the second vehicle.

Exercise 25M: Gender-Neutral Language

1. The operator of the vehicle left the scene without identifying herself or himself.

2. When determining the status of a child as Indian, the state court must seek verification of the child's status from either the Bureau of Indian Affairs or from the child's tribe.

3. Evidence of other offenses may not be admitted as proof of the charged offense if the evidence is relevant only to show the defendant's criminal disposition.

4. A guardian is a person lawfully invested with the power, and charged with the duty, of taking care of another who, for defect of age, understanding, or self-control, is considered unable to administer his or her own affairs.

5. Summary judgment should be denied if the moving party does not sustain its initial burden of proof and if reasonable persons would reach different conclusions from the evidence presented.

6. When requesting that a judgment be set aside, the moving party's attorney must comply with CR 60(e)(1), which requires an affidavit setting forth the facts constituting a defense.

7. The statute gives husbands and wives more freedom to independently dispose of their property by contract, free from court supervision.
OR
The statute gives marital partners . . .

8. Mrs. Edwards is a mother who works outside of the home and who has little time or energy left for her children at the end of the day. Mr. Edwards, on the other hand, operates his accounting business out of his home. Consequently, he is able to give the children the care they need.

9. The Acme Loan Service informed Mr. and Mrs. Valdez that the liens would have to be removed before they could secure a loan.

10. "It is the purpose of this subchapter to assure a meaningful disclosure of credit terms so that the consumer[s] will be able to compare more readily the various credit terms available to . . . [them] and avoid the uninformed use of credit, and to protect the consumer[s] against inaccurate and unfair credit billing and credit card practices." 15 U.S.C. § 1601(a).

11. Rule 9 of the Admission to Practice Rules provides that qualified law students, law clerks, or law school graduates may be granted a limited license to practice law if they 1) have completed at least two-thirds of a three-year course of studies, 2) have the written approval of their law school dean, and 3) have certified that they have read and are familiar with the Rules of Professional Conduct.

12. Helene Russell was a pharmacist in Baton Rouge, Louisiana, when a federal grand jury indicted her on fifteen counts of violating Title 21 U.S.C. §§ 841(a)(1), 841(b)(2), 843(a)(4), and 827(a)(3).

13. The comment to subsection (a) of § 158 explains that a person may invade another's property by "throwing, propelling, or placing a thing" either on the land or in the air above it.

14. The airline's representative claimed that no one could have prevented the tragedy and that the accident was "an act of God."

15. The court may impose an exceptional sentence for the offense of indecent liberties when the victim is particularly vulnerable or unable to resist because of young age and when the offender is not amenable to treatment.

1.   The incident giving rise to the attempted rape charge occurred on November 1, 2009, when the defendant, Harold Strickland went out on a date with Connie Osburn. About 12:30 a.m., Strickland drove Osburn back to his apartment. Once inside, Strickland immediately forced Osburn into the bedroom and onto the bed. Without her consent, he lay on top of her and tried to force his hand under her clothing. Osburn then convinced Strickland that she needed to use the bathroom. He relented and, while she was in the bathroom, Osburn escaped through a window. After finding a police officer, Osburn took her to the scene and showed her Strickland's apartment.

Chapter 27
Grammar

---

1.   <u>If the court allows the prior convictions to be admitted into evidence</u> is a fragment because "if" makes the clause dependent. It should be attached to the preceding sentence.

   Possible revision:

   The defendant's story will not be told if the court allows the prior convictions to be admitted into evidence.

2.   <u>Which generally gives a person worldwide recognition for his or her work</u> is a fragment because "which" makes it a dependent clause. It should be attached to the preceding sentence.

   Possible revision:

   Mr. Barnett won a Pulitzer prize, which generally gives a person worldwide recognition for his or her work.

3.   Both sentences are complete sentences.

4.   <u>The second interest, honor and reputation</u> is a fragment because it lacks a verb.

   Possible revision:

   The second interest <u>is</u> honor and reputation.

5.   <u>Therefore, probably not of probative value to the state's case</u> is a fragment because it lacks both a subject and a verb.

   Possible revision:

   Therefore, <u>they are</u> probably not of probative value to the state's case.

6.   <u>Especially in the light of potential service in New York under the California long arm statute</u> is a fragment because it lacks both a subject and a verb. It should be attached to the preceding sentence.

Possible revision:

Although a technical case can be made for non-compliance with Rule 4(d)(1), the question of the overall efficiency of this approach is open to doubt, especially in the light of potential service in New York under the California long arm statute.

7.   <u>The trend in American courts to balance economic and moral interests in the areas of contract and tort law</u> is a fragment. It lacks a verb.

Possible revision:

The trend in American courts <u>is</u> to balance economic and moral interests in the areas of contract and tort law.

8.   <u>Whether the Los Angeles home is the dwelling house of the defendant</u> is a fragment because "whether" makes the clause dependent. The exception for issue statements does not apply here because this sentence would appear in the text and not be set apart as a formal issue statement.

Possible revision:

The court has only one real issue to decide: whether the Los Angeles home is the dwelling house of the defendant.

9.   <u>Unfair competition, a general term, embracing the narrower area of trademark law, which concerns the same legal wrong, namely, misrepresentations as to the source of goods or services</u> is a fragment because it lacks a verb. "Embracing" is a participle.

Possible revision:

Unfair competition <u>is</u> a general term, embracing the narrower area of trademark law, which concerns the same legal wrong, namely, misrepresentations as to the source of goods or services.

10.   <u>Whereas Ms. Patten alleges that she was robbed</u> is a fragment because of the subordinating conjunction "whereas."

Possible revision:

The defendant states that Ms. Patten gave the coins to him as a gift, whereas Ms. Patten alleges that she was robbed.

EXERCISE 27B: FRAGMENTS

The following are fragments:

-    Which the Hoffelmeirs were emotionally attached to and considered a member of the family

-    Although Mrs. Kravitz tried to shoo the cat away

-    Within 36 hours after impoundment and despite a city ordinance that states that an impounded dog must be held for at least 72 hours before it can be destroyed

<u>*Possible Revision (changes are in boldface)*</u>:

Agnes and Arthur Hoffelmeir were on vacation between October 11 and October 20, 2009. Their neighbors, the Burgesses, offered to take care of their pet cat, **which the Hoffelmeirs were emotionally attached to and considered a member of the family.**

On October 19, 2009, the cat went into Mrs. Kravitz's rose garden and began chewing the rose bushes. **Although Mrs. Kravitz tried to shoo the cat away,** the cat kept returning to the Kravitz yard to chew on the rose bushes. Because this had happened on several other occasions, Mrs. Kravitz called the Humane Society.

The Humane Society impounded the cat, and Mr. Janske of the Society tried unsuccessfully to contact the Hoffelmeirs. The cat was destroyed on October 20, 2009, **within 36 hours after impoundment and despite a city ordinance that states that an impounded dog must be held for at least 72 hours before it can be destroyed.**

The following are fragments:

- If they both were bound by the Sequim City Ordinance

- And because the cat was destroyed before the time provided by the ordinance

- First, that *Sequin* refers to the unlawful garnishment or seizure of property, not the destruction of it

- Second, that they acted within their legal duty when the cat was seized

- Also because Mr. Janske attempted to contact the Hoffelmeirs before the cat was destroyed

- The Society and Mr. Janske being aware that pets are valuable to their owners

- The city ordinance's requirement for a holding period so that pet owners will have an opportunity to claim their pets

- Third, given that the rationale against awarding punitive damages is that an injured party will be adequately compensated through other measures

- And given that the replacement cost of the cat is not adequate compensation

Possible revision (changes are in boldface type):

In *Sequin*, a federal customs official impounded the plaintiff's car and failed to release her car in a timely manner. The court held that if the defendant's conduct could be interpreted as willful or malicious, the plaintiff could recover damages for emotional distress. *Id.* at 811.

We could argue that **if both the Humane Society and Mr. Janske were bound by the Sequim City Ordinance, they acted unlawfully because the cat was destroyed before the time provided by the ordinance.**

The Humane Society and Mr. Janske may make the following arguments. First, ***Sequin* refers to the unlawful garnishment or seizure of property, not the destruction of it.** Second, **they acted within their legal duty when the cat was seized.** Third, because they did not intentionally violate the city ordinance **and because Mr. Janske attempted to contact the Hoffelmeirs before the cat was destroyed,** their actions were not willful or malicious.

The Hoffelmeirs could counter these claims with the following arguments. First, the seizure of the cat may have been lawful. The destruction was not. **(The preceding sentence is correct and not a fragment, even though the word "lawful" is elliptical.)** While *Sequin* is concerned with the unlawful seizure of property, the unlawful destruction of property is even more serious. Therefore, the principle of *Sequin* should apply in this case.

Second, the destruction of the cat before the proscribed time period is malicious and willful misconduct. The Society and Mr. Janske **are** aware that pets are valuable to their owners. Mr. Janske should have waited until the Hoffelmeirs were contacted before the cat was destroyed. **(or "Being aware that pets are valuable to their owners, Mr. Janske should have waited until the Hoffelmeirs were contacted before the cat was destroyed.")** The city ordinance **requires** a holding period so that pet owners will have an opportunity to claim their pets. If the Humane Society had abided by the ordinance, the cat would have been claimed, and the Hoffelmeirs would not have suffered this loss.

Third, given that the rationale against awarding punitive damages is that an injured party will be adequately compensated through other measures **and given that the replacement cost of the cat is not adequate compensation**, the only way the Hoffelmeirs will receive adequate compensation is through an award of damages that includes compensation for mental anguish.

Finally, there is persuasive authority to support the Hoffelmeirs' argument for damages for mental anguish. In a Louisiana case, a neighbor trapped the plaintiff's pet cat and brought it to the animal control center where the cat was destroyed. The plaintiffs sued to recover damages for the mental anguish and humiliation they suffered from the loss of their cat. The court held that if the plaintiffs suffered actual damages, they could be compensated for their mental anguish. *Peloquin v. Calcasier Parish Police Jury*, 367 So.2d 1246, 1251 (La. App. 1979).

EXERCISE 27D: VERB TENSE

1.   The issue in *Farny* **was** whether the New Jersey address **was** the dwelling house or usual place of abode of the defendant. (Use simple past tense for the facts of an analogous case when you do not have to differentiate between the time when the facts occurred and the time when the court proceedings occurred.)

2.   In *Farny,* the plaintiff **contended** that the New Jersey address **continued** to be defendant's dwelling house or usual place of abode. (Use simple past tense for the facts of an analogous case when you do not have to differentiate between the time when the facts occurred and the time when the court proceedings occurred.)

A-45

3.   Correct as is. Use simple present tense for general truths.

4.   Correct as is. Use simple past "held" and "was permissible" for court proceedings; use past perfect "had asked" for facts of analogous case.

5.   Just as the "present" may be a fraction of a second or several centuries long, the "simple past" may include the time period of both the facts and the court proceedings, or it may include just the court proceedings, depending on how the writer sets the sentence up. The sentence is correct as is, if the writer decided to make both the court proceedings and the facts of the analogous case in the simple past. See the following charts.

                              time period
                          of court proceedings
                      and facts of analogous case

If, however, the writer feels that it would help the reader to differentiate between the times of the court proceedings and the facts, simple past tense should be used for the court proceedings and past perfect tense should be used for the facts.

```
___x_____x_____x_____
  facts              court                  the
  of analogous       proceedings            present
  case
```

Possible Revision:

In *Kraus*, the court held that the showup had not been impermissibly suggestive when the victim of an attempted robbery **had been** asked to identify the suspect after the police brought the suspect to the victim's place of business and when the police **had** conducted a pat-down search of the suspect in front of the victim.

6.   Correct as is. Use present tense to express a general truth.

7.   In *Bishop*, the court analyzed the predecessor to the current assault statute and concluded that aiming or discharging a firearm **is** not a lesser included offense of second degree assault. (Use present tense for a general truth.)

8.   Correct as is. Although the verb tense changes three times in this one sentence, from simple present to simple past to past perfect, the changes all correctly correspond to changes in time.

9.   Correct as is. "Held" and "must be read" are simple past tense; "had been written" is past perfect tense.

10. Officer Thompson arrived at the scene of an accident in which a car towing a small trailer **had gone** over an embankment. (Past perfect needed for second verb.)

EXERCISE 27E: VERB TENSE

In 1976, Bob Rhumb built the Cummings's house. In May 1977, Rhumb **built** a garage and fence, and John Miller **bought** the lot north of Rhumb's lot--the lot that is now Walker's--and **built** a house on it that was completed toward the end of 1977. When Rhumb finished building his garage and fence, he **planted** his lawn, which extends* along a line from the fence to the street. Rhumb did not plant the three-foot strip that is now in dispute.

In the spring of 1978, Miller **planted** that strip with grass after Rhumb agreed to pay for a portion of the costs. In addition, along the back portion of his property, Miller **planted** a garden that extends[1] onto the three-foot strip. From the time that Miller planted the lawn and garden in 1978 up to the present, he and the subsequent owners **have maintained** the garden and **mowed**[2]** the grass on the strip that is now in dispute.

During the time that he had owned the property, Rhumb never **discussed** the true boundary line with anyone, except for references to it on two occasions: once, in 1978, when he agreed with Miller to pay a portion of the grass seed costs, and again in 1993, during Kaiser's ownership, when Kaiser was out washing his car, he said something to Rhumb like "Hey, you oughta come over and wash my car 'cause I always mow your lawn."

In January 1998, the Kaisers sold the property to the Hemstads. The Hemstads **lived** there until 2002 and then **rented** the house from 2002 until 2005, when they **sold** it to Debbie Walker. Walker and her predecessors have all maintained the garden and mowed the lawn just as the Millers did.

In 2009, our client, Charlie Cummings and his wife Anna **bought** the house previously occupied by Bob Rhumb. Cummings wants to remodel the house and replace the original garage, but the structure will be located about three feet north of the existing garage and fence. Debbie Walker has protested that the new structures, as described by our client, will be partially built on her property. Cummings has pointed out that the real property line **was located** three feet north of the existing garage and fence, but Debbie Walker is attempting to obtain title by claiming adverse possession.

---

[1] Use present tense "extends" if the lawn and garden are still to this day performing this action; use "extended" if the action was completed in the past.

[2] It is not necessary to write "have mowed." The "have" from "have maintained" carries over to the "mowed."

EXERCISE 27F: SUBJECT-VERB AGREEMENT

1.   were   See Rule 4. *All* refers to the plural *justices*.

2.   were   See Rule 8. Delayed subject is *acts*.

3.   has   See Rule 1. The intervening words introduced by *as well as* do not make the subject plural.

4.   are   See Rule 8. Normal word order is inverted for emphasis. *Parts* is the subject.

5.   has   See Rule 5. The members of the collective noun *majority* are acting as one unit.

6.   is   See Rule 4. *All* refers to the singular *evidence*.

7.   claims   See Rule 1. The intervening words do not make the subject plural.

8.   is   See Rule 7. The verb agrees with the subject *problem*, not the subject complement *employees*.

9.   was   See Rule 9. Words used as words are considered singular.

10.   considers   See Rules 1 and 5. The intervening words do not make the subject plural. Collective nouns acting as one unit, here *appellate court*, are singular.

11.   raise   See Rule 1. *Injuries* is a plural subject; the intervening words do not change its number.

12.   are   See Rules 2 and 7. The plural subject, *Reversing . . . and remanding . . .*, requires a plural verb. The verb agrees with the subject, not the subject complement, *only proper course of action*.

13.   is   See Rule 1. *Case* is the subject.

14.   was   See Exception B to Rule 2.

15.   has   See Rules 3 and 4. The verb must agree with the part of the subject after *nor*, which is *any*, a singular indefinite pronoun.

16.   are   See Rule 1. *Procedures* is the subject.

17.   has   See Rule 1, especially the Note. *Affidavit* is the subject.

18.   publishes   See Rules 9 and 10. *Which* refers back to the title of a magazine, which is always singular.

19.   refers   See Rule 9. *Prior unrelated matters* are words used as words.

20.   was   See Exception B of Rule 2.

EXERCISE 27G: PRONOUN AGREEMENT

1.   <u>See Rule 4</u>. *Appellate court* is a collective noun acting as one unit; consequently, it requires the singular pronoun *it*, not *they*.

2.   <u>See Rule 1</u>. *Witness* is singular, so it requires a singular pronoun. Possible corrections include replacing *their* with *his or her* or changing *a witness* to the plural form *witnesses*.

3.   <u>See Rule 3</u>. *Someone* is an indefinite pronoun that requires a singular pronoun. *His* is singular, but it suggests that all obscene phone callers are male. Replace *his* with *his or her*.

4.   <u>See Rule 1</u>. *Plaintiff* is singular, so it requires a singular pronoun. Possible corrections include replacing *their* with *his or her,* changing *plaintiff* to the plural form *plaintiffs*, or replacing *their* with *a*.

5.   <u>See Rule 1</u>. *Tax consultant* is singular, so it requires a singular pronoun. The best correction is to change *tax consultant* to the plural form *tax consultants*. Changing the pronouns *they* and *them* to singular would require a rather awkward *he or she* and *him or her*.

6.   <u>Correct</u>. <u>See Rule 2</u>. The pronoun *their* agrees with the nearer antecedent *companions*.

7.   <u>See Rule 4</u>. *Board* is a collective noun acting as one unit; consequently, it requires the singular pronoun *its*, not *their*.

8.   <u>See Rule 3</u>. *Somebody* is an indefinite pronoun that requires a singular pronoun. Replace *their* with *his or her*.

9.   <u>Correct. See Rule 1</u>. *Parents and their daughter* is a plural subject requiring a plural pronoun.

10.   <u>See Rule 4</u>. *IRS* is a collective noun acting as one unit; consequently, it requires the singular pronoun *it*, not *they*.

11. <u>See Rule 1</u>. The writer of this sentence managed to make the first set of pronouns *he or she* agree with the singular noun *party*, but then used the plural pronoun *their* later in the sentence. However, replacing *their* with *his or her* would make the sentence awkward. The best correction is to replace *party* with *parties* and *he or she* with *their*.

12. <u>See Rule 4</u>. *Harrison Tractor Company* is a collective noun acting as one unit; consequently, it requires the singular pronoun *it*, not *they*.

13. <u>Correct. See Rule 1</u>.

14. <u>See Rule 4</u>. *Jury* is a collective noun acting as one unit; consequently, it requires the singular pronoun *its*, not *their*.

15. <u>See Rule 1</u>. *Polygraph examination* is singular, so it requires a singular pronoun. The best correction is to replace *they* with either *polygraph examinations* or *such examinations*.

16. <u>See Rule 3</u>. *Everyone* is an indefinite pronoun that requires a singular pronoun. Replace *their* with *his or her*.

17. <u>See Rules 2 and 4</u>. The plural pronoun *they* does not agree with the nearer antecedent *friend*. To correct this sentence and make it more readable, begin by replacing *team* with *teammates*. Now, following the note in Rule 2, reorder the subject of the sentence so that it reads *neither his friend nor his teammates*. Now *they* correctly agrees with *teammates*. (The verb should also be changed to *are*.)

18. <u>See Rule 4</u>. *Court* is a collective noun acting as one unit; consequently, it requires the singular pronoun *it*, not *they*.

19. <u>See Rule 1</u>. Although the singular pronoun *his* agrees with the singular antecedent *perpetrator*, it suggests that the perpetrator leaving fingerprints on the window is male. Replace *his* with *his or her*.

20. <u>See Rule 1</u>. *Person* is singular, so it requires a singular pronoun. Possible corrections include replacing *their* with *his or her* or changing *person* to the plural form *persons*.

1. Howard Davis claims that the apartment manager yelled "Stop!" but never made an effort to interfere.

    or

    Howard Davis claims that he never made an effort to interfere, although he heard the apartment manager yell "Stop!"

2. Davidson cooperated in the search by telling the police about the money and plane ticket under the false bottom of his suitcase. Davidson asserts that the ticket was from a recent trip to California. (If *it* is supposed to refer back to both the money and the plane ticket, then this sentence has an agreement problem [see section 7.4] and should be revised as follows: Davidson asserts that both were from a recent trip to California.)

3. Two brothers, Earl and Mason Hargrove, own two lumber yards, Eastside Building Supplies and Hargrove Lumber and Hardware. Both men are financially stable.

    or

    Both lumberyards are financially stable.

4. O'Brien jammed the coins back behind the car seat and then hid the guns under the spare tire. After a brief search of the vehicle, the coins (or the guns) were found by Officer Martinez.

    or

    O'Brien jammed the coins back behind the car seat and then hid the guns under the spare tire. After a brief search of the vehicle, both the coins and guns were found by Officer Martinez.

5. Juror Marc Stein stated to all other jurors that he had discussed the accident with his brother-in-law, a professional truck driver, who said that the accident could not have occurred as the defendant testified. OR Juror Marc Stein stated to all other jurors that he had discussed the accident with his brother-in-law, a professional truck driver. Stein added that the accident could not have occurred as the defendant testified.

6. After giving chase, Officer Conner apprehended Helman, who had a red bandanna scarf wrapped around a hand with some glass fragments in it.

    or

    After giving chase, Officer Conner apprehended Helman. Wrapped around Helman's hand was a red bandanna scarf containing some glass fragments.

7. A claim by Stravinski that he was not present at the scene of the crime is not necessarily antagonistic with a claim by McDonald that Stravinski was present but did not commit the crime.

    or

    Stravinski claims that he was not present at the scene of the crime, and McDonald admits to being present at the scene of the crime but denies committing the crime. These two claims are not necessarily antagonistic.

8. After conducting a pat-down search of the defendant, Deputy Peterson found a razor blade wrapped in a tissue under his own patrol car.

    or

    After conducting a pat-down search of the defendant, Deputy Peterson found a razor blade wrapped in a tissue under   the defendant's vehicle.

9. Edna Lino testified that several men, including James Crowell, approached the petitioner after he slapped her. She further testified that the petitioner appeared to be afraid that Crowell would beat him up.

    or

    Edna Lino testified that several men, including James Crowell, approached the petitioner after he slapped her. She further testified that Crowell appeared to be afraid that the petitioner would beat him up.

10. Clyde Reeves and his son, Daryl, were both injured in two automobile accidents that occurred within two months of each other. The first accident occurred on October 8, 2008, when Clyde was injured in a rear end collision with a vehicle driven by Melvin Maye. Clyde immediately sought and received medical care for the injuries from Dr. Charles Santino, his family physician. Later, on November 10, 2008, while still under Dr. Santino's care, he was involved in an accident with a vehicle driven by Carter Szabo. Clyde again sought and received medical treatment from Dr. Santino.

1. In *Colorado Carpet*, the court held that an oral contract for ordinary carpet was unenforceable. The *Colorado Carpet* court reasoned that there was no evidence to indicate that the carpet was specially made for the buyer because it could be found in other retail outlets. The defendant tried to use this reasoning to say that the towels, like the carpet, are not special.

2. The defense could bring up evidence of large sales of happy face items during the happy face fad several years ago. However, the happy face fad no longer exists, a fact that weakens this argument.

    or

    This is a weak argument, however, because the happy face fad no longer exists.

3. When the defense counsel addressed the subject of silence during direct examination of the defendant, she opened the door for a further development of the subject.

4. The trial court admitted the defendant's prior convictions for theft because they proved only that the defendant acted in conformity with his propensity to commit crimes. ER 404(b) prohibits admitting evidence for such a reason.

5. The destruction of the rosebushes could be classified as permanent. Such a classification would make the school district liable for the difference in the value of the Archers' property before and after the damage.

6. The Washington State Constitution expressly forbids the in-court questioning of witnesses about their religious beliefs for the purpose of affecting the weight of their testimony. Wash. Const. art. I, § 11. This absolute prohibition is repeated and underscored by Washington Rule of Evidence 610.

7. In the present case, the prosecution asked the prosecuting witness several questions about her religious activities, beliefs, and opinions, bolstering her credibility with the jury at the expense of Mr. Doughtery's due process rights. (RP 151-52). U.S. Const. amend. XIV; Wash. Const. art. I § 22. In allowing this line of questioning, the trial court committed an error of constitutional magnitude. *See Thomas*, 130 Ariz. at 435-36, 636 P.2d at 1217-18; *Estabrook*, 162 Or. at 101, 91 P.2d at 850.

8. Thus, the prosecution used the witness's religious beliefs, which had nothing to do with the issues before the trial court, to make her testimony seem more credible than Mr. Dougherty's testimony. Such use of religious beliefs is prohibited under Const. art I, § 11 and ER 610. (Note that *which* is correctly used to introduce a nonrestrictive clause.)

9. Under ER 609(a)(2), when a trial court admits prior   conviction evidence of a crime that does not contain an element of deceit, fraud, or false swearing, the trial court commits an error of constitutional magnitude. *State v. Harris,* 102 Wash. 2d 148, 685 P.2d 584 (1984). The rationale for this rule is that while crimes of dishonesty bear directly on a defendant's propensity for truthfulness, other types of crimes do not bear on truthfulness and their admission might serve to prejudice the jury against the defendant.

10. The trial court did not give a cautionary accomplice instruction. This court held that such an instruction is required whenever the prosecution relies solely on accomplice testimony.

EXERCISE 27J: PRONOUN ANTECEDENTS

1. The Bloomquists' pre-marital agreement states that Mr. Bloomquist's residuals are community property.

2. Freeman discusses numerous rules of usage in his book, *The Grammatical Lawyer.*

3. From the minutes of the board, we can infer that it knew about the structural weaknesses in the building and decided not to act.

4. Notes made by an attorney during a client interview must be protected under the work-product rule; otherwise, the opposition will have access to the strategy he or she plans to use in the case.

5. The petitioner testified that he did not deliberately shoot anyone.

EXERCISE 27K: PRONOUN REVIEW

1. In *Finch*, the petitioner's vehicle collided with the respondent's. The petitioner submitted a claim for property damage to respondent's insurance carrier, which the respondent agreed to pay.

2.   Anita Hempstead is a single mother with an 18-month-old daughter. The lights and noise from the night baseball prevent the child from sleeping. This annoyance occurs twice a week. Consequently, Ms. Hempstead claims that the loss of sleep interrupts the child's entire weekly schedule.

3.   Upon receipt of Wilson's case, the prosecutor's office treated it in the same fashion as all other referrals. That treatment included processing the police reports, screening them for legal sufficiency, typing and filing an information, and setting an arraignment date with proper notice. Once the prosecutor realized that it could not be routinely processed in the twelve business days between receipt of the police reports and Wilson's eighteenth birthday, he referred the case to the adult division for filing charges.

4.   In May of 2009, the president of Glad Tidings Towel Company (GTT) telephoned the president of Smokey Stover Hotels (SSH). The president of GTT said, "I am now responsible for the order." He also told the president of SSH that GTT had completed 20,000 of the 50,000 towels ordered. This information surprised the president of SSH because he had never signed a contract ordering the towels and because it is company policy that the SSH president sign all contracts for orders.

EXERCISE 27L: MODIFIER PLACEMENT

1.   **Just** the deputy prosecutor asked that the plaintiff describe his assailant.
         No one but the deputy prosecutor asked.

     The deputy prosecutor **just** asked that the plaintiff describe his assailant.
         She did not demand or require.

     The deputy prosecutor asked **just** that the plaintiff describe his assailant.
         She asked for only one thing.

     The deputy prosecutor asked that **just** the plaintiff describe his assailant.
         Only the plaintiff, no one else should do the describing.

     The deputy prosecutor asked that the plaintiff **just** describe his assailant.
         Just describe, not draw or point out or name.

     The deputy prosecutor asked that the plaintiff describe **just** his assailant.
         Just the assailant, no one else should be described.

2.   **Only** the defendant claims that the plaintiff was sleeping.
       No one else makes this claim.

      The defendant **only** claims that the plaintiff was sleeping.
       He claims it but cannot prove it.

      The defendant claims **only** that the plaintiff was sleeping.
       He claims only one thing.

      The defendant claims that **only** the plaintiff was sleeping.
       No one else was sleeping.

      The defendant claims that the plaintiff was **only** sleeping.
       Only asleep, not dead

EXERCISE 27M: MODIFIER PLACEMENT

1.   After Mr. Harper pays alimony and child support, he has **barely** enough money to live on.

2.   The court stated that the unavoidable accident defense was appropriate **only** when neither party was at fault and when the party was surprised by sudden changes in circumstances that the party could not reasonably anticipate.

EXERCISE 27N: MISPLACED MODIFIERS

1.   The deputy marshal testified that a copy of the complaint was served on the defendant at his Chicago residence on March 12, 2009.

      or

      The deputy marshal testified **that** on March 12, 2009, a copy of the complaint was served on the defendant at his Chicago residence.

2.   The duty of a plaintiff in a failed vasectomy is to mitigate damages **only** through a reasonable means; an abortion is not required.

      or "only duty of a plaintiff"

3.	The court reasoned that, **given the chance**, many people would be willing to support the unplanned child.

	or

	The court reasoned that many people, given the chance, would be willing to support the unplanned child.

4.	Acme Clothing Co. discriminated against Mary Smith when it failed to issue her a new credit card **under her maiden name** for an existing open-ended account.

5.	Custom-made towels **imprinted with yellow happy faces trimmed in purple and ordered by the buyer** satisfy the requirement of specially manufactured goods.

6.	Harrison Lumber Co., the plaintiff in this action, has filed suit **in federal district court** against our client, Lloyd Putnam, for breach of contract.

7.	Hawaii currently does not restrict foreign investment in privately owned real estate; on the contrary, discrimination **based on ancestry** is prohibited in real estate transactions.

8.	In *Rovinski v. Rowe*, Robert Rowe brought a personal injury action against Stanley Rovinski for injuries **that he sustained** from an automobile accident.

9.	Mrs. Davidson's car collided with Mrs. Howe's car, which was traveling at a lawful rate of speed, **in the middle lane**.

Poor Q

Unclear whose car was in middle lane

10.	The court held that the photographs, **although gruesome,** must be considered in light of the facts needed to be proved by the prosecution.

## EXERCISE 27O:	DANGLING MODIFIERS

1.	In order to answer this question, the court must examine the rule that governs service of process.

2.   Applying the majority rule to our facts, the court will find that the benefit of the Bells having a healthy child outweighs the burden.

3.   To prove discrimination, Ms. Smith must show that the only difference between her and the others granted credit was Ms. Smith's protected classification.

4.   In using the balancing test, the court must consider whether the defendant testified at the prior trial.

5.   Comparing *McDonald* to our case, the court will find that the facts are conclusive that Komotios's identification in the police car resulted from impermissibly suggestive police actions.

     or

     Comparing *McDonald* to our case, the court will find that Komotios's identification in the police car resulted from impermissibly suggestive police actions.

6.   In measuring monetary damages to real property, courts make two distinctions. *factors*

7.   In determining what constitutes "appreciable time," the courts have not clearly defined a specific or standard amount of time.

8.   Equipment designs are presented to the prospective buyer for approval. Once the design is approved, a bid stating the contract price is submitted.   *passive*

9.   If you wish to collect your pruning fee from Mr. Brown, filing a lien against his orchard may be the best course of action.

EXERCISE 27P: PARALLELISM

1.   The defense counsel elicited that the appellant paid for a listed telephone in his own name, kept some clothes and artifacts there, and had a room there that was ready for him to occupy. (The key words, *paid, kept,* and *had*, must match.)

2.   As a result of the collision, Rice has suffered a severe concussion, two broken ribs, a lost front tooth, whiplash, and numerous bruises and lacerations. (*Tooth* is now the key word, and it matches *concussion, ribs, whiplash, bruises and lacerations*.)

3.   Provisions allowing arbitration are generally upheld because they enhance fair dealing among the parties and prevent litigation. (*Enhance* is parallel with *prevent*.)

6. To determine whether Azore discriminated against our client, the court must examine four factors.

4.   Chavaria's only reasons for breaking into the locked box in the Senator's desk were his suspicion that it contained the Senator's financial records and his expectation of a probable reward from the Justice Department.

       or

       Chavaria's only reasons for breaking into the locked box in the Senator's desk were that he suspected that it contained the Senator's financial records and that he expected a probable reward from the Justice Department.

5.   The voluminous record in this case contains both substantial and conflicting evidence regarding the sequence of events, the actions of the parties, and the condition of the intersection.

6.   The issues for review are whether the trial court abused its discretion by not placing a value on certain items of personal property and by ordering John to pay $600 per month in child support for his four children. (*By not placing* matches *by ordering.*)

7.   One factor governing the award of child support includes the cost of caring for, maintaining, and educating the children.

       or

       One factor governing the award of child support includes the cost of the care, maintenance, and education of the children.

8.   The two critical factors in the "instrument or agent" analysis of Fourth Amendment search and seizure law are the government's knowledge and acquiescence in the search and the intent of the party performing the search. (The nouns *knowledge* and *acquiescence* match *intent.*)

9.   Clipse described the assailant as wearing a green denim outfit and glasses and having short wavy hair. (The key words *wearing* and *having* are parallel.)

10.   To ensure that claimants would be aware of the new act, the Legislature directed the Department of Ecology to publish a statutorily prescribed notice by four different means: 1) **publishing** the notice once a year for five years in major as well as local newspapers; 2) **publishing** the notice every six months on radio and television stations broadcasting in every county; 3) **posting** the notice in a conspicuous location in every county; and 4) **including** a copy of the notice with notices of taxes due for 1972 mailed by each county treasurer.

1.   The trial court concluded that the agreement was not only economically but also procedurally fair.

2.   Green fibers that were found to be microscopically indistinguishable from the fibers in Nichol's t-shirt were found both in the car and on the gloves.

3.   Mr. Parker claims that the trial court's actions resulted in a property distribution that was neither fair nor equitable.

4.   The plaintiff alleges that the City not only failed to erect proper warning signs but also failed to trim obscuring vegetation at the northeast quadrant of the intersection.

     or

     The plaintiff alleges that the City failed not only to erect proper warning signs but also to trim obscuring vegetation at the northeast quadrant of the intersection.

5.   The jury is not to consider this evidence as either proof of negligence or an admission of negligence on the part of the City.

     or

     The jury is not to consider this evidence either as proof of negligence or as an admission of negligence on the part of the City.

6.   The notation on the agent's copy could mean that Peters either made only a quote to Garfield or actually obtained the excess coverage from Munson Insurance.

7.   The State can neither take action that will unnecessarily "chill" the assertion of a constitutional right nor draw adverse inferences from the exercise of a constitutional right.

8.   In this case, the prosecutor's comments appear to extend more to the defendant's theory of mistaken identity than to his guilt or innocence.

9.   The State charged Mookins with one count of assault committed either by using a weapon or instrument likely to produce bodily harm or by knowingly inflicting grievous bodily harm upon the victim.

10. Heller did not object to the use of the medical records evidence either at the board hearing or during the trial de novo in superior court.

Chapter 28
Punctuation

1.   . . . by counsel, but he moved . . . .

2.   . . . in the courtroom, and petitioner . . . .

3.   . . . was 21, but he disputed . . . .

(No comma after *and* because *and* joins two dependent *that* clauses.)

4.   No comma needed.

(The *and* joins two dependent *that* clauses, not two independent clauses.)

5.   . . . billing practices, yet he expressed . . . .

(Use of a semicolon before *yet* is also permitted.)

6.   . . . Mafia connections, and one has . . . .

7.   . . . against him, and the record reflects . . . .

8.   . . . was $17,000, and its street . . . .
        or
        . . . was $17,000 and its street . . . .

(Acceptable to omit comma because clauses are short and closely related.)

9.   . . . minimal, for it was Jones . . . .

10.   . . . false story, but the *Times* . . . .

1. To convict the defendant of the crime charged, the court must find that he had actual knowledge that he was possessing stolen property. **(Comma sets off an introductory infinitive phrase.)**

2. In response to DuPont's request, Hommel agreed to accompany DuPont to the rear of the store **(Comma sets off prepositional phrases.)**

3. Viewing the evidence in a light most favorable to the prosecution, the trial court found for the defendant. **(Comma sets off introductory participial phrase.)**

4. In the early morning hours of December 3, 2009, officers from the Houston Police Department were dispatched to an abandoned railroad depot. **(Comma sets off two introductory prepositional phrases. Comma would also be required after complete date. See rule 9.)**

5. Furthermore, the trial court cautioned the jury to scrutinize separately each defendant's case. **(Introductory transitional word must be set off by a comma.)**

6. Moreover, to ensure that claimants would be aware of the new act, the legislature directed the Department of Ecology to publish a statutorily prescribed notice. **(First comma sets off transitional expression; second comma sets off introductory infinitive phrase.)**

7. If there is probable cause police may extend a search without a warrant to containers in cars. *California v. Acevedo,* 500 U.S. 565 (1991). **(Comma sets off an introductory dependent clause.)**

8. In *Beck*, the United States Supreme Court held that the death sentence may not constitutionally be imposed for a capital offense when the jury was not permitted to consider any lesser included offenses. **(Although the prepositional phrase is short, most legal writers set off case names.)**

9. After waiving his right to a speedy trial six times, Martin pleaded guilty to the crime of indecent liberties. **(Comma sets off an introductory combination of two prepositional phrases.)**

10. However, if the evidence is admissible for one of these purposes, the trial court must determine whether the danger of undue prejudice from its admission outweighs the probative value of the evidence. **(First comma sets off a transitional expression; second comma sets off an introductory dependent clause.)**

EXERCISE 28C: COMMAS

1. Of the twenty, two witnesses are willing to testify. **(Comma needed to prevent reader from seeing *twenty-two* as a unit and assuming that a long introductory phrase was opening the sentence.)**

2. During a surveillance, on three successive evenings . . . . **(Presumably, the police observed people exchanging cash for packaged articles on three successive evenings, not that the surveillance occurred on three successive evenings. If the latter is intended, the comma should be placed after *evenings*.)**

3. Two years before, the car's brakes failed on a steep mountain road. **(Comma needed to prevent reader from initially assuming that this is a long introductory dependent clause.)**

4. Once, he had the idea that all women were laughing at him behind his back. **(Comma needed to prevent reader from initially assuming that this is a long introductory dependent clause.)**

5. Without a doubt, about half the witnesses to the accident will be unwilling to get involved. **(Comma needed to prevent reader from assuming that *without a doubt about half the witnesses to the accident* is a long introductory phrase.)**

28D: COMMAS

1. Trooper Yessler, who investigated the accident, testified that the "primary causal factor" of the accident was Neimeyer's intoxicated state. **(Trooper Yessler is completely identified by his name. *Who investigated the accident* adds additional information, not restricting or limiting information, so add commas.)**

2.   The state trooper who investigated the accident testified that the "primary causal factor" of the accident had been Neimeyer's intoxicated state. (**Who investigated the accident is restrictive; it limits the meaning of state trooper, so no commas.**)

3.   The Washington State legislature enacted RCW 28A.605.020, which requires school districts to develop a policy to allow parents to access their child's school. (**The number of the act identifies it completely. The nonrestrictive clause adds important additional information, but that information does not restrict or limit the meaning of RCW 28A.605.020.**)

4.   The police talked with a neighbor who had seen a man matching Daniels's description within a block of the Wyatt home on the day of the burglary. (**Who had seen a man . . . restricts the meaning of neighbor, so no commas.**)

5.   At about 10:30 p.m., Officer Underwood encountered Norman Rhemn, whom she had observed driving by several times during the evening. (**Whom she observed driving by several times during the evening adds important additional information to the sentence, but that information does not restrict or limit the meaning of Norman Rhemn, so add commas.**)

6.   Did the trial court err in giving instruction 9, which sets forth the circumstances permitting the jury to find whether the petitioner had "actual knowledge" that he possessed stolen property? (**Instruction 9 is completely identified; the which clause adds important information to the sentence, but that information does not restrict or limit the meaning of Instruction 9, so add a comma.**)

7.   Those who fail to file waive their water rights. (**Who fail to file restricts or limits the meaning of those, so no commas are needed.**)

8.   The defendant's conviction was reversed on the ground that the informant was a material witness who could not be subpoenaed by the defense. *Id.* at 1146. (**This sentence has two restrictive clauses: 1) that the informant was a material witness and 2) who could not be subpoenaed by the defense. The first restricts the meaning of ground; the second restricts the meaning of witness. No commas needed.**)

9. The State appealed to Division Two of the Court of Appeals, which reversed and remanded in a published opinion filed August 5, 1986. **(The name of the court identifies it completely; the *which* clause adds information that is important to the sentence, but it does not restrict the meaning of *Division Two of the Court of Appeals*, so add a comma.)**

10. A polygraph examination is a reasonable extension of those statutory conditions that require a probationer to follow the instructions of his or her probation officer. *See, e.g.*, Wash. Rev. Code 9.95.210. **(*Those statutory conditions* is restricted or limited by the *that* clause, so no comma is needed.)**

EXERCISE 28E : COMMAS

1a. Only those independent contractors who performed the actual dredging are responsible for any negligence.
1b. All independent contractors performed the actual dredging, and all are responsible for any negligence.

2a. Defense counsel will discuss only those factors that favor exclusion of prior conviction evidence.
2b. Defense counsel will discuss all the factors, and all the factors favor exclusion of prior conviction evidence.

3a. There is only one serial number, and it is missing.
3b. There is more than one serial number, but the police are checking only for the one that is missing.

EXERCISE 28F: COMMAS

1. The State has charged the defendant with dealing in a controlled substance, a Class B felony. **(Rule 5: *A Class B felony* is a nonrestrictive appositive for dealing in *a controlled substance*.)**

2. . . . motion, arguing that . . . . **(Rule 6: Comma sets off nonrestrictive participial phrase.)**

3. The only witness, Ann Peters, had discussed her potential criminal liability with the prosecutor. **(Rule 5: *Ann Peters* is a nonrestrictive appositive for *only witness*.)**

4.   . . . constitutionally invalid, Lemons . . . . **(Rule 6: Comma sets off beginning participle, *contending that his* prior guilty pleas were constitutionally *invalid*.)**

5.   (Rule 6: No commas added. *Decision* is modified by the restrictive participial phrase, *affirming his conviction*. If a comma is added after decision, then the sentence means that the Petitioner affirms his own conviction.)

6.   Olson claims that a new trial should have been granted because Nyles, the victim, was available to testify. **(Rule 5: *Nyles* is a nonrestrictive appositive for *victim*.)**

7.   Correct as is. **(Rule 5: *Thomas and Scalia* are not the only Supreme Court Justices, so they are restrictive appositives.)**

8.   Campbell's most recent conviction was for second-degree assault, the same crime he is currently charged with committing. **(Rule 5: The comma sets off the nonrestrictive appositive.)**

9.   Holding that the facts were sufficient to require the submission of the defense of duress to the jury, the Court of Appeals reversed, stating that "[t]he time has come when we can no longer close our eyes to the growing problem of institutional gang rapes in our prison system." **(Rule 6: Both participial phrases, *holding that the facts were sufficient to require the submission of the defense of duress to the jury* and *stating that "[t]he time has come when we can no longer close our eyes to the growing problem of institutional gang rapes in our prison system* are nonrestrictive.)**

10.   . . .Court of Appeals, assigning error . . . . **(Comma sets off nonrestrictive participial phrase and tells reader that Olsen, not Division Two of the Court of Appeals, is assigning error in the appeal.)**

EXERCISE 28G: COMMAS

1.   . . . replied, "Sure." **(Rule 8: Comma separates introductory words from quotation.)**

2.   One could infer, therefore, that the billing procedures were there for her to see. **(Rule 7: *Therefore* is an interrupter that needs to be set off by commas.)**

3.   . . . "yes," then . . . . **(Rule 8: Commas go inside closing quotation marks.)**

4.   No commas added. **(Rule 8: Quotation is preceded by *that*.)**

5.   Roberts, however, asserts that she was amenable to process at all times. **(Rule 7: *However* is an interrupter that must be set off by commas.)**

6.   Other cases, on the other hand, suggest that the evidence necessary to satisfy the second prong of the *Workman* test may come from any source. **(Rule 7: *On the other hand* is an interrupter that must be set off with commas.)**

7.   No commas added. **(Rule 8: *That* precedes quotation.)**

8.   Add a comma after *concluded*. **(Rule 8: Comma separates introductory words from quotation.)**

9.   An appellate court may, on its own initiative or by motion of a party, request additional evidence before rendering a decision on a case. **(Rule 7: The compound interrupting phrase, *on its own initiative or by motion of a party* is set off with commas.)**

10.   In *Alford*, the United States Supreme Court held that a plea of guilty is constitutionally valid, in spite of a defendant's claim of innocence, when there was strong evidence of guilt before the trial court and when the plea was a voluntary and an intelligent choice among the alternative courses of action open to a defendant. 400 U.S. at 37-38. **(Rule 7: *In spite of a defendant's claim of innocence* interrupts the sentence, so it must be set off with commas.)**

EXERCISE 28H: COMMAS

1.   Yesler later identified James in a photo montage, in a lineup, and at trial. **(Rule 10: Commas are needed to separate items in a series.)**

2.   The evidence shows that the defendant was only present at the crime scene, not "ready to assist." **(Rule 9: Comma sets off the contrasting phrase.)**

3. The prosecutor's comment of disbelief was directed at the defense theory of mistaken identity, not at the credibility of a witness. **(Rule 9: Comma sets off contrasting phrase.)**

4. Thompson pulled his gun, held it straight up in the air, and told Lew not to bring anyone back. **(Rule 10: Commas are needed to separate items in a series.)**

5. Thus, the 90-day "time for trial" rule under CrR 3.3(c)(1) began to run when Lewis was arraigned, not when the State filed the information. **(Rule 9: Comma sets off contrasting phrase.)**

6. The sanity commission concluded that Thomas was incapable of perceiving the nature of his conduct at the time of the offense, was unable to distinguish right from wrong, but was competent to stand trial. **(Rule 10: Commas are used to separate items in a series. Also note that the last item in the series is a contrasting element.)**

7. The court must follow United States Supreme Court decisions, not a decision by the New Mexico Court of Appeals, when determining whether a defendant is a public or private figure. **(Rule 9: Pair of commas set off contrasting phrase.)**

8. The *Harris* court held that such an instruction is required whenever the prosecution relies solely on accomplice testimony, but that failure to give the instruction is not reversible error when there is sufficient corroborating testimony. **(Rule 9: Comma sets off contrasting element.)**

9. Chavez saw a man on the ground, but was unable to identify him because of the darkness. **(Rule 9: Comma is used to set off contrasting element.)**

10. Jeffreys was arrested for armed robbery, yet was also charged later with second degree burglary. **(Rule 9: Comma needed to set off a contrasting element.)**

EXERCISE 28I: COMMAS

1. She was taken into custody on May 11, 2009, and arraigned on May 12, 2009. **(Rule 12: Comma follows the day and year when a full date is used and the sentence continues after the date.)**

2.   The documents in question mysteriously disappeared from the Dallas office on December 2, 2008, only to reappear in the office in Clovis, New Mexico, on December 9. **(Rule 12: Comma follows full date when sentence continues. Comma follows city and state when sentence continues. Sentence is also revised to avoid the awkward *Clovis, New Mexico, office*.)**

3.   Bennett purchased twelve acres of remote, undeveloped land in central Florida in 1997. **(Rule 11: Comma separates coordinate adjectives.)**

4.   Secret, unexpressed intentions are irrelevant. **(Rule 11: Comma separates coordinate adjectives.)**

5.   Each applicant was required to enclose a self-addressed, stamped envelope with the application form. **(Rule 11: Comma separates coordinate adjectives.)**

6.   Johnston moved to Las Vegas, Nevada, in February 2006 to attend school. **(Rule 12: City and state are separated by commas and a comma follows state when sentence continues. No comma between partial date.)**

7.   The publisher mailed the contract on 1 March 2008 to the author at her address in Cincinnati, Ohio.   **(Rule 12: No comma when date is in inverted order. The sentence is also revised to avoid the awkward *Cincinnati, Ohio, address*.)**

8.   "Substantial evidence" exists if it is "sufficient to persuade a fair-minded, rational person of the truth of the declared premise." *See Davis v. Microsoft Corp.,* 149 Wn.2d 521, 531, 70 P.2d 126 (2003). **(Rule 11: Comma separates coordinate adjectives.)**

9.   Peterson filed his motion to vacate on October 26, 2008, more than two years after the trial court entered the judgment of acquittal. **(Rule 12: Comma after full date because sentence continues.)**

10.   People who received one of these letters were told to "mail $5.00 to the last name and address on the list," which was Amy Andersen, 1813 South Washington, Lawrence, Kansas 66044, or they would suffer "bad luck and other misfortune." **(Rule 12: Commas are used to set off individual elements in an address. Comma after zip code when sentence continues.)**

1. . . . the blue, another 100 hits. **(Rule 14: The comma indicates the omission of "envelope contained.")**

2. . . . criminal findings, each based . . . . **(Rule 13: *Each based on the same prior convictions* is an absolute.)**

3. . . . Jerome's, namely, proceed under . . . . **(Rule 15: Some writers may prefer to use a dash before *namely*.)**

4. . . . ; that is, he or she . . . . **(Rule 15: Comma sets off expression that introduces explanation.)**

5. . . .--that is, without a valid will-- . . . . **(Rule 15: Comma sets off expression that introduces an explanation.)**

6. Melvin Andersen is listed as the president of the corporation; Philip Andersen, the vice-president of operations; Teresa Andersen, the vice-president of internal affairs, and Mary Andersen, the treasurer. **(Rule 14: The commas indicate the omission of *is listed as*.)**

7. . . . cut off, Irene . . . . **(Rule 13: *Her only source of income cut off* is an absolute.)**

8. . . . valuable possessions, *e.g.*, a three-carat diamond, ... **(Rule 15: Comma sets off an expression to introduce an example.)**

9. . . . labelled "successful," Glenda . . . . **(Rule 13: *Her surgery having been labelled successful* is an absolute. Also note that the comma goes inside closing quotation marks.)**

10. . . . calls, the first . . . . **(Rule 13: *The first less than two hours after the incident* is an absolute.)**

1. Omit comma before *if*. **(*If* introduces a restrictive adverbial clause.)**

2. Omit comma before *when*. **(*When* introduces a restrictive adverbial clause.)**

3. Correct as is. (*Because* **introduces a restrictive adverbial clause.**)

4. Omit comma before *as*. (*As* **introduces a restrictive adverbial clause.**)

5. No commas needed. (*If* **introduces a restrictive adverbial clause.**)

6. . . . practices, although there is no . . . . (*Although* **introduces a nonrestrictive clause.**)

7. Omit comma before *unless*. (*Unless* **introduces a restrictive adverbial clause.**)

8. Correct as is. (*When* **introduces a restrictive adverbial clause.**)

9. Omit comma before *because*. (*Because* **introduces a restrictive adverbial clause.**)

10. . . . evidence, even though that ruling . . . . (**No comma before** *when* **because it is a restrictive adverbial clause, but a comma is needed before** *even though***.**)

EXERCISE 28L: UNNECESSARY COMMAS

1. The police put a "trap" on the phone, so when the man called the next day, the police were able to trace the call. (**Rule 19: Comma is not needed between a conjunction and an introductory clause.**)

2. The Hoffelmeirs will probably receive not only the replacement value of the cat but also compensation for their mental anguish. (**Rule 18: Do not use a comma to separate correlative pairs.**)

3. Defendants may argue that precisely because the plaintiff operates its business in the small community of Lincoln, it holds a position of special prominence in that community sufficient to make it an all-purpose public figure. (**Rule 20: No comma needed between** *that* **and an introductory clause.**)

4. The fire could reasonably be classified as "manifestly dangerous" because of its intensity, the danger of injury from the propane tanks, and the condition and construction of the barn. (**Rule 17: Omit comma separating subject from verb. Revise sentence to avoid the overly long subject.**)

5.   The *Barr* decision is entitled to much weight in Washington both because it was decided by the full bench of the Washington Supreme Court and because there was no dissenting opinion. **(Rule 18: Comma should not separate correlative conjunctions.)**

6.   Correct as is. **(Rule 18: Correlative conjunctions join main clauses.)**

7.   Wells claims that he was denied his right to cross-examine the representatives of the third-party payors who testified about the payment restrictions. This claim could be valid if he was prevented from negating any inference that he knew the billings were fraudulent. **(Rule 17: Do not separate a subject from its verb with a comma. Revise the sentence to avoid an overly long subject.)**

8.   The court held that when there is a period of delay between filing the information and the arraignment, the time for trial set forth in CrR 3.3(c)(1) begins to run the date the information is filed. **(Rule 20: Do not use a comma between *that* and an introductory clause.)**

9.   The court ruled that although the form was incorrect, the substantive information supplied by the claimant met the legislative intent by "providing adequate records for administration of the state's waters and notifying the State that the water was being put to beneficial use." *Id*. at 704. **(Rule 20: Do not use a comma between *that* and an introductory clause.)**

10.   Correct as is. **(Correlative conjunctions connect two independent clauses.)**

EXERCISE 28M: COMMA REVIEW

1.   The Supreme Court held that summary judgment was proper because the State's actions in failing to perform the eye examination and noting an appropriate restriction were totally unrelated to the accident. **(No comma before restrictive *because* clause, and no comma for pairs, *failing . . . and noting*.)**

2.   At the disposition hearing, the State presented a document describing Nowell's prior criminal history, which consisted of twelve burglary convictions and two minor offenses subject to diversion. **(Comma after introductory phrase is correct; another comma must be added before nonrestrictive clause.)**

3.   Correct as is. **(A comma is needed after the introductory phrase, and commas are needed to set off the nonrestrictive appositive** *an escort service.***)**

4.   Both contentions will fail if this accident resulted without any warning of Ms. O'Toole's impending blackout. **(The comma should be deleted before the restrictive** *if* **clause.)**

5.   Correct as is. **(A comma is needed to set off the transition** *for example*, **and another comma is needed to set off the introductory clause.)**

6.   Even though the evidence does not demonstrate that Marvin and Leroy verbalized any plan to carry out the assault, they both appear to have been active participants in the crime. **(A comma is needed to set off the introductory clause.)**

7.   The first instance of alleged prosecutorial misconduct occurred during closing argument when the prosecutor made several statements concerning O'Toole's failure to call Doris Simms as an alibi witness. **(No comma is needed before the restrictive adverbial clause.)**

8.   Owens asserts that the manufacture of a controlled substance may be accomplished only by extraction or chemical synthesis, not by cultivation. **(A comma is needed to set off the contrasting element.)**

9.   On the evening of February 28, 2010, Atlanta Police Officer Louise Simpson was working undercover on prostitution detail. **(Add commas in full date; no comma is needed to set off restrictive appositive.)**

10.   A waiver to the right to a jury trial must be voluntary, knowing, and intelligent. **(To avoid ambiguity, add a comma before the conjunction connecting the last item in a series.)**

11.   Kevin Morton rode as the "spotter," the person designated to alert the boat driver when the skier falls. **(A comma is needed to set off the nonrestrictive appositive, but it should be placed inside the closing quotation marks.)**

12.   Defense counsel chose to present only one alibi witness, Bertha Owens, who stated that she was in Des Moines, Iowa, at the time of the robbery. **(Commas correctly set off the nonrestrictive appositive, but a comma is needed after the state when more of the sentence follows.)**

13. Marie Tao, the defendant's girlfriend, was contacted by an officer who asked if the defendant was there, but she denied knowing anything about his location. **(Commas correctly set off the nonrestrictive appositive, but a comma must be added before the coordinating conjunction *but* because it joins two independent clauses.)**

14. Mason maintains that, like the convictions in *Mace*, one of his convictions was reversed on appeal and that the habitual criminal finding must likewise be vacated. **(Commas correctly set off the interrupter *like the convictions in Mace*, but the comma between the pair of *that* clauses must be deleted.)**

15. The Barkers argue that even if the statutory notice is constitutionally adequate, they substantially complied with the requirements of the Water Rights Registration Act. **(No comma is needed between *that* and an introductory clause, but a comma is required after the introductory clause.)**

16. Correct as is. **(No comma is needed before *and* because it connects a pair of dependent clauses.)**

17. When Officer Smith asked who had been driving the cars, Pinette approached him and said, "I'm the driver of the Volvo." **(A comma is needed to set off the introductory clause, and another comma is needed to set off the explanatory words from the quotation.)**

18. This court has warned prosecutors that it will not tolerate the admission of repetitious, inflammatory photographs. **(Comma is needed to separate coordinate adjectives.)**

19. The Washington State Supreme Court has held that when a case has been appealed and a judgment issued by the appellate court, the trial court may not interfere "by any proceeding in the cause which is not directed by the appellate order." *State v. Graeber,* 49 Wash. 2d 874, 875, 307 P.2d 563 (1957). **(No comma is needed between *that* and an introductory clause, but a comma is needed after the introductory clause.)**

20. The appellant placed her daughter in a private, out-of-district school in Denver, Colorado, without first notifying the school district. **(A comma is needed to separate the coordinate adjectives, and commas must be added to the geographical name.)**

1. license; therefore,

    (Otherwise the sentence has a comma splice.)

2. act; it
    or
    act. It

    (The clauses are closely related, so the semicolon is preferable.)

3. permission; therefore,
    or
    Correct as is

    (The clauses are closely related, so the semicolon is preferable.)

4. license; however,

    (Otherwise the sentence has a comma splice.)

5. road; Thorndike
    or
    Correct as is

    (When preceding or subsequent sentence are long, it is better to separate main clauses such as these into separate sentences. If sentence length is not a problem, then the writer may want to use the semicolon to juxtapose the contentions of the opposing parties.)

6. defendant; neither
    or
    defendant. Neither

    (The semicolon helps to balance one main clause against the other. A period or full stop before the second main clause gives slightly more emphasis to the second main clause.)

7. house; both
    or
    Correct as is

(If preceding or subsequent sentences are long, it may be better to separate the main clauses into two sentences. The advantage of connecting both main clauses with a semicolon is that it emphasizes the close relationship between the two main clauses.)

8.   observable; he

(Otherwise the sentence has a comma splice.)

9.   . . . cousins; therefore,

(Otherwise the sentence has a comma splice. A colon is also a possible choice. See Section 28.3.)

10.   lane; in *Taylor*,
        or
        Correct as is

(If preceding or subsequent sentences are long, then it is better to separate main clauses into separate sentences. The advantage of keeping both main clauses in the same sentence is that this structure emphasizes the comparing and contrasting of the two fact situations.)

EXERCISE 28O: SEMICOLONS

1.   incorrect -- satisfied; the

(Otherwise the sentence has a comma splice.)

2.   correct --

(Conjunction "but" does not require a semicolon, but one can be used here because the second main clause has internal commas. See section 28.2.2.)

3.   incorrect -- satisfied; however,

(Otherwise the sentence has a comma splice.)

4.   correct --

(The first clause is subordinated by "although," so it is not a main clause.)

5.	correct --

	(The conjunctive adverb "however" occurs in the middle of a main clause, so it is preceded and followed by a comma. The main clauses are correctly separated by a semicolon.)

6.	correct --

	(Main clauses are divided by a semicolon, and the two subordinate "if" clauses are separated from their main clauses with commas. See Rule 2 for punctuation of long introductory clauses.)

7.	incorrect -- search, however,

	(The first sentence is correctly punctuated, but the second sentence is not. Replace the semicolon after "search" with a comma because the second sentence begins with a clause subordinated by "if"; therefore, it is not a main clause.)

8.	incorrect -- admitted; however,

	(Otherwise the sentence has a comma splice.)

9.	correct --

	(Although this version is correctly punctuated, it forces the writer into an overly long sentence. A better solution is to write two sentences. " . . . search. Therefore, the evidence . . . .")

10.	correct --

	(The main clauses are correctly divided and balanced against each other by semicolons.)

EXERCISE 28P: SEMICOLONS

1.	business; the degree . . . another business; and the test of sensibilities, that is, ... **(The last item has internal commas.)**

2.	warrant; injunctions; damages, which are measured by the loss suffered by the plaintiff; or declaratory judgment. **(The third item has internal commas.)**

3.   neighborhood; the ratio . . . tenants; and the possible interference with the tenants' comfortable enjoyment of life, with their right to privacy, and with their use of the property as an apartment. **(The last item has internal commas.)**

4.   requirements, including the special requirement imposed by the waterfront commission; 2) the fitness . . . restaurant; and 3) the activities . . . . **(The items are long, and the first item has internal commas. Note that whether the items are numbered in itself does not affect when to use semicolons; however, writers tend to number items when they are long, and long items generally require semicolons.)**

5.   intoxicated; 2) the driver . . . vehicle; and 3) the motor vehicle . . . . **(Some, if not all, of the items are long and they are enumerated.)**

EXERCISE 28Q: SEMICOLONS

1.   exist; consequently **(Otherwise the sentence has a comma splice.)**

2.   the health . . . child; the weight . . . fetus; available . . . techniques; and the length . . . determined. **(The last item in the series has internal commas, so semicolons are needed to separate the items.)**

3.   non-viable _ because **(No punctuation is required. The second clause, beginning with "because," is a subordinate clause.)**

      For those writers who prefer that the cause come before the effect, the sentence can be revised as follows:

      In *Green*, the court held that viability was a factual issue that must be decided by a jury; consequently, the court refused to rule as a matter of law that a fourteen-week-old fetus was non-viable.

4.   Correct as is. **(Some writers may choose to use a comma before "but" in this sentence, but both main clauses are relatively long and both contain internal punctuation. Consequently, the semicolon before the coordinating conjunction "but" more clearly separates the two main clauses)**

5.   discretion; the court OR discretion. The court .... **(Using just a comma after "discretion" produces a comma splice.)**

6.   reasonable; therefore **(Otherwise the sentence has a comma splice.)**

7.   nuisance; but **(Some writers may choose to use a comma rather than a semicolon here, but both main clauses are rather long and both contain internal punctuation. Consequently, the semicolon before the coordinating conjunction "but" separates the two main clauses more clearly.)**

8.   Correct as is.
      or
      community; public

      (Use of the semicolon is preferable because the main clauses are not overly long and they are closely related. The semicolon also heightens the comparison.)

9.   Correct as is. **(Conjunctive adverb "however" is placed in the middle of a main clause, not in between two main clauses.)**

10.   Correct as is. **(Items in the series are long enough to justify using semicolons. Furthermore, each item is itself a main clause.)**

EXERCISE 28R: COLON

1.   A two-part inquiry is used to determine reliability: 1) was the confrontation procedure suggestive, and 2) under the totality of circumstances, was the identification reliable even if the confrontation procedure was suggestive?

2.   Officials who are accorded absolute immunity seem to share one common characteristic: they make discretionary decisions in an adversarial proceeding under time and information constraints.

3.   Correct. **(No colon needed because the main clause is not a grammatically complete lead-in.)**

      or

      In California, the service-oriented businesspersons subject to the bulk sales law are **the following:** the baker, the cafe or restaurant owner, the garage owner, or the cleaner and dyer.

4.   By requiring independent corroborating evidence only in Miranda situations, the court has adopted what seems to be a radical approach:

admissions made in a pre-Miranda setting, at least in DWI cases, do not need corroborating evidence.

5. Correct **(No colon needed because the main clause is not a grammatically complete lead-in.)**

    or

    The defendant is accused of assaulting **the following victims:** Agnes Miller, Denise Donovan, Ellie Emory, and Christine Fremont.

6. The court found that the prosecutor's comments during closing argument were not improper **for three reasons:**

    (1) the witness was "peculiarly available" to the defendant and would have been able to elucidate the events of the crime;

    (2) the witness has pleaded guilty to a prior crime on the condition that he would not be prosecuted for the crimes charged; and (3) the defendant repeatedly attempted to place responsibility for the charged incident on the witness. *Id.* at 628.

    (Lead-in main clause is now grammatically complete.)

7. An investigation revealed that five individuals were at the railroad depot on the night Jones was assaulted: Francis O'Connor, Noel O'Connor, Phillip Whalen, Paul Mendoza, and Tony Rialto. **(Do not use a semicolon to set up a list.)**

8. Correct.

9. The court in *Petersen* reasoned that a separate covenant is implied between the seller and purchaser "because of the unusual dependent relationship of the vendee to the vendor." *Id.* at 1158. **(No colon because quotation is integrated into writer's sentence.)**

10. For the court to have found for the plaintiffs in *Kelley*, the plaintiffs would have had to establish **the following:**

    (1)   the condominium conversion required "extensive rehabilitative construction";

    (2)   the defects complained of by the condominium owners were defects of the "new" construction; and

(3)   the defects complained of were "latent" defects.

EXERCISE 26S: APOSTROPHES

1.   judge's error. See rule 1.
2.   judges' error. See rule 3.
3.   prosecuting attorney's assistant. See rule 4.
4.   son-in-law's employer. See rule 4.
5.   its. See rule 6.
6.   Terry and Howard's children. See rule 5.
7.   Terry's and Howard's children. See rule 5.
8.   Lois's complaint. See rule 2.
9.   fringe benefits' value. See rules 3 and 4.
10.   two weeks' vacation. See rule 3.

EXERCISE 28T: APOSTROPHES

1.   agencies'
2.   Mathewses'
3.   securities'
4.   Davises'
5.   bar examiners'

EXERCISE 28U: APOSTROPHE

1.   100's. See rule 8.
2.   prostitutes' clientele. See rule 3.
3.   electricians' union. See rule 3.
4.   franchi<u>se</u>' <u>s</u>ecurities. See rule 2 on voicing three *s* sounds.
5.   Doris's and Thomas's executors. See rules 2 and 5.
6.   for old times' sake. See rule 2.
7.   change the <u>Mary's</u> to <u>Mari's</u>. See rule 8.
8.   promissory note's validity. See rule 1 and 4.
9.   policies' effects. See rule 3.
10.   tenants' organization. See rule 3.
11.   Schultz's automobile. See rule 1.
12.   Schultzes' automobile. See rule 3.
13.   bosses' meeting. See rule 3.
14.   the Mayor of New York's statement. See rule 4.

15. Clinton & Nelson's construction company. See rule 5.
16. 1990's. See rule 8.
17. justice of the peace's decision. See rule 4.
18. too many *if*'s. See rule 8.
19. somebody else's problem. See rule 4.
20. whose. See rule 6.

EXERCISE 28V: OTHER MARKS OF PUNCTUATION

1. Correct

2. According to the *ALWD Citation Manual* and the *Bluebook*, this quotation is not long enough (34 words) to be single spaced and indented.

3. Do not use an ellipsis when the omission occurs at the beginning of a quotation.

4. Do not use quotation marks around long quotations that are singled spaced and indented.

5. Using the standard enunciated in *Berenson*, the *Kurzius* court held that "[a] zoning ordinance will be ***

   or:

   Using the standard enunciated in *Berenson*, the *Kurzius* court held the following: "A zoning ordinance will ***

EXERCISE 28W: HYPHENS

1. Correct

2. non-stock corporation

3. Correct

4. six-month lease

5. Correct

6. ex-husband

7. Correct

8. all-inclusive report

9. Correct

10. fact-finding commission

11. priest-penitent privilege

12. low- to moderate-income housing

13. Correct

14. Correct

10. cross-examination

EXERCISE 28X: COMMA SPLICES AND FUSED SENTENCES

1. Correct

2. Comma splice

Corrected:

Mr. Cratchett bought the property sometime in 2009. The facts are in dispute as to the specific month.

3. Fused sentence

Corrected:

Before Mr. Cratchett bought the property, it was owned by Mrs, Moriarty, who died in October 2008.

4.   Comma splice

Corrected:

Since 2002, the Kearneys have used the property in a variety of ways; for example, they have regularly mowed the grass in the disputed area since 2002 or 2003.

5.   Correct

6.   Correct

7.   Comma splice

Corrected:

When the Kearneys built the patio area, they did not ask Mrs. Moriarty for permission, and Mrs. Moriarty did not object to their use of the area before or after the patio was built.

8.   Correct

9.   Correct

10.   Comma splice

Corrected:

Mr. Cratchett believed that the boundary line between the two properties was the retaining wall that had been mistakenly extended onto Mr. Moriarty's property; however, in October 2009, he had his land surveyed and learned the true property line.

Chapter 31
English as a Second Language

---

1.   housing = non-count
      home = count

2.   employment = non-count
      privacy (not privacies) = non-count

3.   furniture (no "s") = non-count; change "were" to "was"
      refrigerator = count

4.   electricity = non-count
      water = non-count when used to refer to the running water in a home; can be a count noun when used to talk about the water in a particular lake, river, or area (the "waters of Lake Michigan" or the "coastal waters of Mexico")

5.   traffic = non-count
      transportation (no "s") = non-count; change "were" to "was"

Officers Tony Marino and Enrique Garcia were on **(no article)** patrol in **a** new housing development when they noticed **(no article)** two boys loitering near **a** group of rural mailboxes. One of the boys had his back turned toward the officers, and he appeared to be opening **an** envelope. The other boy appeared to be putting **(no article)** several pieces of mail in **a** backpack. When Officer Marino stopped the patrol car and started to get out, **a** third boy who was further down the street, shouted, "Run!" The two boys near the mailboxes dropped the mail and started running into **an** orchard on the outskirts of the housing area. Officer Marino ran after them. While in **(no article)** pursuit, Marino saw the second boy throw the backpack behind **an** apple tree.

1.   "on patrol" → no article because it is an idiom

2.   "a new housing development" → article used because "development" is a singular count noun and this was the first time it was mentioned

3.   "two boys" → no article because of the noun marker "two"; see exception to Rule 1

4. "a group" → article used because "group" is a singular count noun and this was the first time it was mentioned

5. "an envelope" → article used because "envelope" is a singular count noun and this was the first time it was mentioned; "an" is required because "envelope" begins with a vowel sound

6. "several pieces" → no article needed; "several" is a noun marker; see exception to Rule 1

7. "a backpack" → article used because "backpack" is a singular count noun and this was the first time it was mentioned

8. "a third boy" → article used because "boy" is a singular count noun and this was the first time the third boy was mentioned; note the difference between "three boys," which does not take an article and "a third boy," which takes an article

9. "an orchard" → article used because "orchard" is a singular count noun and this was the first time it was mentioned; "an" is required because "orchard" begins with a vowel sound

10. "in pursuit" → no article because it is an idiom

11. "an apple tree" → article used because "tree" is a singular count noun and this was the first time it was mentioned; "an" is required because "apple" begins with a vowel sound

Exercise 31C: Articles--"A" or "An"

1. Cosmic Toys, Inc. will be found liable for an act of negligence if the plaintiff can prove that it knew that its Little Tommy gun was hazardous to children.

    or:

    Cosmic Toys, Inc. will be found liable for negligence if the plaintiff can prove that it knew that its Little Tommy gun was hazardous to children.

2. If the court does not admit a piece of evidence, the Cosmic report on injuries sustained by children playing with the Little Tommy gun, the plaintiff's case will be seriously compromised.

    or:

If the court does not admit evidence of the Cosmic report on injuries sustained by children playing with the Little Tommy gun, the plaintiff's case will be seriously compromised.

3.   The plaintiff must prove that Cosmic had knowledge that when the gun replicated the backfire of an actual weapon, some children sustained eye injuries.

or:

The plaintiff must prove that Cosmic knew that when the gun replicated the backfire of an actual weapon, some children sustained eye injuries.

4.   In addition to the Little Tommy gun, Cosmic makes guns that are toy versions of ones used when hunting.

5.   One Cosmic toy rifle, known as NRA Junior, is made of wood and plastic.

6.   Cosmic has recalled the NRA Junior because, with extensive outdoor use, the wooden stock of the toy rifle suffered deterioration, including warping and splintering.

or:

Cosmic has recalled the NRA Junior because, with extensive outdoor use, the wooden stock of the toy rifle deteriorated, including warping and splintering.

7.   The defendant expects testimony at trial that Cosmic has a record of recalling toys it knows to be defective.

8.   The defendant will argue that Cosmic recalls toys only when it is under intense pressure to do so by consumers and the media.

9.   Research about Cosmic and other toy gun manufacturers gives the industry a mixed report card.

10.   The study noted that Cosmic was accused of discrimination against its female employees.

or:

The study noted that Cosmic was accused of discriminating against its female employees.

The reasons for adding or omitting "the" are in italics after each instance. The numbers of the reasons coincide with the reasons in Chapter 30 in The Legal Writing Handbook, 5th edition and Chapter 10 in Just Writing, 3rd edition.

1. On Tuesday, April 11, 2008, Jonny Phan was driving home from his new job at the [*reason 2 — phrase restricts identity*] Sears store in the [*reason 4 — shared local knowledge*] Queen City Mall.

2. Unfortunately, the [*reason 3 — noun preceded by ranking adjective*] quickest route home was through an area known as the [*reason 2 -- phrase restricts identity*] "red light district."

3. When Phan stopped at an intersection, two women who had been standing near the intersection [*reason 1 — noun "intersection" has already been used once*] waved to him.

4. The [*reason 3 — noun preceded by ranking adjective*] taller woman leaned into an open window on the [*reason 4 —shared universal knowledge; reader knows cars have a passenger side*] passenger side of the [*specific identity of noun is clear to reader even though the noun "car" has not actually been stated yet; it was inferred in sentence 1*] car and asked him "if he wanted to have some fun."

5. Phan, who has difficulty understanding [*"the" omitted; reason — rule 4; plural noun meaning all of a class*] American accents, was not sure that he understood her correctly.

6. Assuming the [*reason 1 — noun "women" has already been used once*] women might be in trouble or need help, Phan pulled over to the curb.

7. The [*reason 3—noun preceded by ranking adjective*] taller woman told him that an hour with them would cost $100.

8. Convinced now that the [*reason 1—noun "women" has already been used*] women needed help Phan reached into his wallet and handed them a $5.00 bill.

9. Officer Peter Meyers, who was on bicycle patrol in the area, saw the [*specific identity of noun is clear to reader even though the noun "money" has not actually been stated yet; it was inferred in sentence 8*] money exchange hands.

10. Stopping his bike on the [*reason 4 — shared universal knowledge; reader knows cars have a driver's side*] driver's side of the car, Officer Meyers immediately arrested Phan for soliciting prostitution.

In June 2009, Dr. Arminda Sanchez was interviewed by Dr. Jorge Padilla for **a** position at Five Rivers Community College teaching in **the** history department. When Dr. Sanchez asked Dr. Padilla why she was being interviewed, he replied that **the** interview was granted because **the** department "had to interview women." Dr. Sanchez said that response hit her "like a punch in the stomach." At **the** time, **the** history department had only male faculty. After **the** interview, Dr. Padilla offered Dr. Sanchez **a** probationary teaching position, which she accepted. She became **the** first female hired by **the** department in sixteen years.

In **the** summer of 2009, Dr. Sanchez arrived at **the** history department and noticed that she was surrounded by artwork in **the** department hallways depicting semi-nude women. Because she was **the** only female faculty member in **the** department, she immediately felt uncomfortable. She was also afraid **the** pictures would make her female students feel uncomfortable, so she took them down and filed **a** complaint with Dr. Walter Bade, **the** department chair. According to Dr. Bade, **the** pictures were put up in **the** hallway by Dr. Padilla only one week before Dr. Sanchez's arrival. Dr. Bade reported **the** incident to Dean Norma Gernon. He also forwarded **the** complaint to Dean Gernon.

Dean Gernon determined that **the** artwork was "not sexually harassing"; nevertheless, she issued **a** new policy expressly forbidding posting sexually explicit material. In response to Sanchez's complaint, Gernon told Sanchez that Sanchez was being "baited" by Dr. Padilla. She recommended that Sanchez withdraw **the** complaint and "try to get along" with her colleagues.

Despite **the** new policy, one week later, Dr. Padilla put up several more posters of nude women in **the** history department hallway. Several female students and **a** female faculty member from **the** music department complained about **the** posters. Feeling that she was being sexually harassed, Dr. Sanchez asked if her classes and office could be moved to another building. Dr. Bade agreed that **the** classes could be moved, but he stated that **a** faculty member must have **an** office in his or her own department so Dr. Sanchez's office could not be moved.

By **the** middle of **the** fall semester, Dr. Sanchez and Dr. Padilla had met several times to resolve their differences. In **the** first meeting, Dr. Padilla insisted that pornography "was liberating to women" and argued that only **an** unenlightened individual would complain about artwork. In **the** second meeting, he listened to Dr. Sanchez for **a** few minutes and then abruptly stood up, said "the department was better to a man before you came," and then left **the** room. In their final meeting, Dr. Padilla told her that **a** good colleague would not complain about small things such as **a** few posters and that she needed **a** man in her life "to loosen her up."

Two days after **the** final meeting with Dr. Padilla, Dr. Sanchez filed **a** formal complaint of sexual harassment with Dean Gernon and **the** Equal Employment Opportunity Commission (EEOC).

Exercise 31F: Auxiliary, or Helping Verbs

1. States **can** be sued for damages for not making courthouses accessible to persons with disabilities.

2. In its 2005 ruling on Washington State's sentencing guidelines, the U.S. Supreme Court decided the juries, not judges, **must** consider each fact that could lengthen a prisoner's sentence.

3. The sentencing guidelines decision **could** affect thousands of prison sentences.

4. Although federal judges have a lifetime appointment, they **can** be impeached for misconduct.

5. In the past, Senators **would** filibuster when they lacked the votes to prevent confirmation but they believed that a president's judicial nominee was unsuitable.

Exercise 31G: Base Form of Verbs

1. When the Supreme Court disqualified a constitutional challenge to the phrase "one nation under God" in the Pledge of Allegiance, it did not **rule** on the issue of whether the phrase violated the constitutional ban on establishing an official government religion. *(base form of the verb used with "did")*

2. The lawsuit was **brought** by a father who was an atheist and who objected to his daughter having to say the Pledge of Allegiance in school. *(past participle form of the verb used with "was")*

3. Because the father did not have custody of the daughter, the court could **disqualify** the challenge because the father did not have legal standing to bring the suit. *(base form of the verb used with "could")*

4. United States district court and court of appeals judges follow a code of ethics with guidelines about when they should **disqualify** themselves from hearing a case. *(base form of the verb used with "should")*

5. In contrast, Supreme Court justices determine for themselves when, based on a conflict of interest, they will **recuse** themselves from a case. *(base form of the verb used with "will")*

6.   In 2005, Sierra Club attorneys questioned whether Justice Antonin Scalia could **remain** impartial on a case involving Vice President Cheney after Scalia and Cheney went on a hunting trip together. *(base form of the verb used with "could")*

7.   Scalia issued a 21-page memo explaining that he had not **discussed** the case with Vice President Cheney. *(past participle form of the verb used with "had")*

8.   The case involved access to meeting records from the Bush administration's energy task force that was **headed** by Vice President Cheney. *(past participle form of the verb used with "was")*

9.   In a 7-2 vote, the Court decided that Vice President Cheney was not **required** to turn over records from the energy task force meetings. *(past participle form of the verb used with "was")*

Following the decision, Chief Justice William Rehnquist appointed a committee that will **study** procedures for handling ethics complaints against federal judges. *(base form of the verb used with "will")*

Exercise 31H: Verbs with Gerunds and Infinitives

1.   In 2004, the Supreme Court ruled that the 1998 Child Online Protection Act appeared **to violate** the constitutional right to free speech.

2.   The authors of the Act intended **to prevent** children from viewing sexually explicit material on the internet.

3.   Web site operators could avoid **paying** fines of up to $50,000 by requiring users to prove they were adults.

4.   The Act permitted adults **to access** the sexually explicit material if they used a credit card.

5.   Because the ruling was a 5-4 vote, the federal government may attempt **to bring** the case to trial again in lower court.

or:

Because the ruling was a 5-4 vote, the federal government may attempt **bringing** the case to trial again in lower court.